KISSING WHALES
HEALING DOLPHINS

AQUACRANIAL THERAPY AND THE
CETACEA BLEU BABIES

D0943322

REBECCA GOFF

Outskirts Press, Inc.
Denver, Colorado

Kissing Whales
Healing Dolphins
AquaCranial Therapy and the Cetacea Bleu Babies
All Rights Reserved
Copyright © 2005 Rebecca Goff

Outskirts Press
http://www.outskirtspress.com

ISBN-10: 1-59800-137-X
ISBN-13: 978-1-59800-137-2

Outskirts Press and the "OP" logo are trademarks belonging to
Outskirts Press, Inc.

Printed in the United States of America

FOREWORD

It was the dolphins that first told me to do Craniosacral Therapy on infants and children to age three in the ocean. They said it would allow the physical body to hold higher levels of consciousness. So, a few friends volunteered their children and we headed into the wide-open ocean with wild dolphins. I asked an osteopath, Dr. John Upledger, what he thought about what we were doing, when meeting him a few years later. He said it made absolute sense to him. I find that everything the dolphins tell me makes sense whenever I run their theories past experts in the field. The dolphins initially taught me how to move the sutures in the skull. When I asked a teacher for input on a question regarding sutures, on the second day of an introductory Cranial Sacral Therapy course, he gave me a very surprised look.

"You do not get into that until about the seventh year of training," he said.

"Well, I am working on babies tomorrow and this is what I plan on doing. I just need this one technical answer, if you could possibly help me."

Bless Malte for answering my questions. He is an awesome teacher. He brought the first disarticulating skull I had ever seen into class. I can see inside of peoples' bodies and know what the bones look like and the precise alignment, as proven by x-rays taken later. I am not into cadaver courses. We are talking dead bodies now; sometimes just dead heads. Playing with the plastic skulls, taking them and putting them to-gether—that is fun. We do get some interesting looks from the tourists, so colorful, with flowers around their necks and vivid flowers printed on their shorts and swimsuits. Here we are with a bunch of cute, tiny children, next to the always "postcard perfect" ocean, on one of the most beautiful strips of sand on the planet - playing with assorted bones and skulls. Many times, there are also screaming children. Sometimes, they just scream. Then I look at them and let out a scream. Excitedly, children answer me with another scream, and on it goes, until the game wears out and we do something else. A considerable amount of tension is released with the screaming.

After rotating a mover and shaker in the film industry during a treatment, and telling him to scream when upside down, face under the ocean water, he said, "That was excellent. I should do it more often."

I feel the pent-up energy of a person who has been in situations that just make them want to scream, and of course, they cannot. So, the energy builds and stays within the body. Another time on that same discreet Four Seasons golden beach, covered with lounge chairs and cabanas, four feet into the glistening water, a woman began screaming and crying—only not face down in the water! Even at the adjoining Grand Wailea Resort, some tourists asked what was going on.

"Oh that is just someone having a release during the dolphin treatment," was the casual answer from the beach attendant.

By the next day, guests were asking if I had heard the "dolphin" release screaming and could they have a release? Having a release was the most exciting thing on the menu for the next couple of weeks. Information travels like wildfire on the guest wireless. If one experiences a great treatment, half the hotel will be asking for it the next day. I have experienced a deluge of white-robed, polished beauties pouring over the spa desk, trying to reserve one of the sought-after appointments.

Sometimes the screaming is the trauma being released from children. Even when the screaming and crying includes words echoing down the beach in German, my name being screamed in the middle of it all is very clear. Worried tourists ask the lifeguards if I regularly hurt children at the beach. The tanned and toned local boys just laugh.

"She helps all the kids, island kids, all over the world kids. There, look."

The tourists will turn to see the child who was just moments ago in the throws of agonizing screams, now smiling and hugging me or handing me a cookie. Not all children scream during sessions, in case you are wondering. Not what I expected when dolphins told me to do consciousness work. I was a political activist and environmental activist years ago. I realized that the thing needing to happen for anything else to be effective would be a change in consciousness. I devoted myself to being a consciousness activist.

In the seventies, I choreographed my aerobics classes to music that I had recorded, so that the most political songs played when the mind was the most open, which was during the hardest physical part of the routine. When you are doing your best to keep that leg moving up and down, even though it feels as if you could not possibly kick it into the air one more time, you are focused. Your mind is open. Ever do hypnosis as a kid at slumber parties? I was twelve, my friend eleven, in our flannel, flowered pajamas, some sparkly piece of Mom's costume jewelry in hand, I was asking my friend where she would like to "go."

"I want to see my brother," she bubbled, bouncing on the bed, smiling so happy. "I miss him."

"Okay," I say, and begin to wave the sparkly treasure at the end of the chain rhythmically back and forth in front of her eyes. "Keep your eyes on the diamond. You are beginning to relax," I say seriously, mimicking the hypnotist from the Ed Sullivan show, my voice low. I continue to "play" hypnotist.

Suddenly, I am with her, in her mind. We are in a field in Vietnam. It is in our minds, but we are really there somehow, even though we are still sitting on the ruffled bedspread at the slumber party. Her brother is there. We saw so many brothers, all in uniforms, all so young. Guns were firing, something exploding, screaming, blood everywhere, and so much movement. We had no idea; we were still naïve'. .

I quickly brought her back with "One, two, three, open your eyes," but the emotional devastation caused by her experience in trance was now part of her reality.

It took three hours of hard work to stop her hysterics. I began studying psychology right then, in seventh grade. Consciousness still fascinates me. The tissue in the body has consciousness, the organs also. When I was a child and was asked what I wanted to be when I grew up, my first choice was an inter-dimensional scientist. I am continually amazed by the scope of this reality. The dolphins have certainly stretched my awareness.

With AquaCranial Therapy, many times the results are not what anyone expected. I had a woman referred to me for a problem stemming from forceps damage. I could see why the referring therapist would have considered that a cause, but my subtle perception indicated the chin became "stuck" on some part of the womb or pelvis during the birth process and was then "pulled." The client "felt" that this explanation resonated with her. Her jawbone would straighten and then pull back out of alignment when an emotion would rise to the surface. After several treatments, she remembered the details surrounding her birth and her mother's pregnancy. Apparently, her mother had a hysterectomy before becoming pregnant. Who knows what butchered space this little baby had developed in. Since she is in her sixties, the operation her mother had was long, long ago. Mom did not know that she was pregnant until the end of the pregnancy. Why would she? She had a hysterectomy, no chance of more kids, right? No wonder my client had issues around not being wanted or supported in her birth process.

After she "remembered" these details, her chin held in place when it moved into alignment. The unusual thing was that the client was also no longer afraid of the dark! During intake questioning at her first appointment, she gave me all of her symptoms, aches, pains, surgeries, etc. At the end, she laughed and flippantly added, "Oh yes and I am afraid of the dark, if you can do anything about that."

She came to see me for three or four treatments a trip, three times a year. She arrived very excited for her second treatment series. Her husband had pointed out to her that they were leaving the blackout shades all the way down and she was sleeping in complete darkness. The shades were normally lifted an inch or two when they returned home from trips. Miss needed to be able to see outlines around things, as she was terrified of total darkness. She and her husband looked at everything she had been doing when the change occurred and they said it had to be the treatments with me. Later, during her time with me, she would get in the ocean and float all alone, something else she swears she would never have done before therapy. She is not the first to move past fears of the water during ocean treatments. Sometimes, the client comes specifically to heal past trauma around the water. Some have almost drowned, or even actually drowned and been brought back. Others have a fear of unknown origin. I always chat a bit on the way into the ocean with clients, and ask if there are any issues around water for them.

One woman told me, "The last time I left this beach it was on a gurney with a sprained neck from the waves slamming me into the sand. That is why I have so much back pain. I figured you could cure me of the trauma as well as the back pain. You are famous, aren't you?"

Once, I was doing a deluxe foot treatment on a client. While he was lying back, feet luxuriously soaking in special mineral water with orchids floating around the bowl, I massaged his head. He asked what I was doing when I incorporated a couple of cranial sacral movements. When I told him, he bolted upright on the table.

"You are Rebecca, You created the AquaCranial treatment. I knew you before you existed. You are famous in LA." I loved that, "I knew you before you existed." It was definitely an inter-dimensional scientist kind of compliment.

I fell in love with his girlfriend too. I did not know she was his girlfriend until later. This woman was totally awesome. So cute. She had the most unusual spinal swaying, like scoliosis that was turned in toward the spine instead of going side to side. She said it was what gave her the sashay when she walked. This girl could sashay from birth, no doubt. Her second time for treatment, she told me that she knew I had moved her bones because she could no longer get her body to pop. Seems she would twist and gyrate and her body would pop loudly all over the place prior to treatment. I have more fun with some of the people who find their way to my table. Once, the wife of a professional baseball team owner wanted her husband to hire me for the team so I would be available for her. I will not live anywhere that doesn't have plenty of sun and an ocean you can actually swim in (with whales and dolphins, of course). So, I say no when people ask me home with them.

Men in their early thirties, who were active in sports, have decompressed as much as 3-inches during a series of treatments.

One client went back to the mainland for Christmas and his parents exclaimed, "Dan, you have a neck!"

There was the man who had one leg 2-inches shorter than the other. This causes all kinds of physiology problems, and using a lift in the shoe does not help the misalignment in the hips. At the end of the treatment, two even legs and a balanced pelvis later, the client asked who was going to pay for the new alterations to his clothes. Seems all his designer duds had been altered to fit the shorter leg! (No, I did not cover the cost of alterations).

One poor 19-year-old arrived for a table treatment, all bent over and shuffling along in obvious pain. She had been in the hospital for two weeks with an "unknown pelvic disease." After multiple Demerol shots for the pain, her body hurt so much from the shots that her parents told the doctors she was better, checked her out of the hospital, and brought her to Hawaii. Her right hip was about an inch and a half higher than the left hip. After an evaluation of her body, when I questioned her, she admitted to standing often with one leg up on a chair, (when doing dishes), up on the toilet, (when brushing her teeth), up on the dashboard, (when driving), etc. She had simply misaligned her hip. Fifty minutes later, she was out the door, pain-free, and excited to swim with dolphins.

It is all like a puzzle to me, listening to what the body has to say and peeling away the layers of pain, stress, accidents, emotions, and misalignment. I love assisting in releasing and discovering both the cause of the challenges, and the blessings of health underneath. I was once told "the bigger the challenge, the bigger the blessing," and I have received both extremes in following the dolphins and whales. Blessings are when I have taken one person at a time into an ocean bay, and swum out to the dolphins, while many times holding the client by the hand, for their first-time experience of looking into the eyes of these beautiful, conscious beings. I have each client lie down with a pillow under his or her head, and I treat them with dolphins swimming around, until I swim them all the way back to shore--Wild dolphins that have come to show and teach us much, while remaining free.

Back at the shore, I awaken the client, help him or her off with their wetsuit and wrap them in warm, dry towels. I then leave them to rest on a lounge chair in the company of my favorite pool and beach staff. Then I swim back out to the dolphins, before, between, and after clients—hours at a time, several days a week, for months. They sonar me, teach me how to do some of what they do, and they heal me. Some days, they show me a glimpse through a crack in realities of what is yet to come. I have been swimming with dolphins for years, logging thousands of hours.

Guests of one resort, along with employees, would watch from the cliffs as the dolphins obviously came to us. Resort guests would come up to me saying, "Wow, most hotels keep their dolphins in pools. This is way cooler."

As I cruised past children I had been swimming with earlier, surrounded by dolphins, I would smile and call out, "What did we learn in the ocean?" and the children would shout out, "Keep all dolphins free! Keep all dolphins free!"

Some days, people would watch to see if the dolphins actually arrived with me. They did. Many days they left with me too. Dolphins and whales call me all over the islands, all over the world.

We are opening a research, treatment and training facility in the South Pacific to be in the water, free from harassment, with the whales we love so much. Perhaps, I will see you there someday.

In the meantime, this little book is a mix of case histories, therapist training stories, recommendations, and a bit about the whales and dolphins that train me.

Enjoy.

TABLE OF CONTENTS

CHAPTER 1
THE BABY HOSPITAL

How did this happen? I watched the tiny baby who was struggling so hard to breathe. Eight weeks early, at a week old, he still weighed less than 4-pounds—up less than a pound in a week. Many preemie babies have undeveloped lungs, but this was different.

"I know he would be better if you could just touch him," his mother had said, oh so softly into the phone the day before.

I flew straight over to see him. They say a preemie's lungs will never develop, but I disagree to a certain extent. If it is already a blueprint in the biological system, therapy does help development after birth. Something was wrong here. I had perceived it immediately when I spoke with his mama on the phone, and now, here, touching him, it was the same. It was as if the genetic code had been disturbed, the pathway to the next step mutated. Later, his mama would remark that she knew there was a problem by what I would not say.

Her firstborn, a miracle baby had been treated by me when he was hours old, and she knew me very well. This baby's oxygen saturation had gone up 2 points in a week. After 6-hours of continuous treatment in his incubator, it went up six more points. It moves, of course, but there is a point around which it stabilizes. What I had perceived in his lungs, the doctor confirmed, was a lung disease. He had not told the mother before my arrival. I asked later, and found it usually comes from the mother, or others close during her pregnancy, smoking cigarettes. The condition was never expected to improve.

This girl was a good Mama. Cigarettes are legal aren't they? Even doctors and nurses smoke them; so how bad can they be really?

I watched the tiny baby struggle so hard it tore at your heart. Maybe he would survive, but you did not even know if that was what you wanted, when you watched his body racked with the stress of simply trying to breathe. A roomful of monitors, sad parents, sick babies, beep, beep, beep, buzzing, alarms; soft waves and whale sounds would have been so helpful. Some hospitals use music, and they have proven it to be beneficial.

I truly believe, and prove, treating infants in warm water with underwater sounds is amazing—easily incorporated into hospital settings, and we would see more miracle babies.

Now, my eyes constantly moved up to the tiny infant's monitor, watching every beat of his heart, noting his ability to breath and how each touch shifted the levels of numbers and jagged lines. Never let him relax too much; don't let the baby drift into it, as you normally would. It is so different with these beings that still belonged in the womb. I never took my hands off of him that first day, except when they made me leave while they did something with one of the other children.

There were several babies in here, flown in emergency ambulance helicopters or special planes across the ocean from all over the Hawaiian Islands and even farther away: Guam, Tonga. I moved aside while a doctor showed a nurse how to position another baby for x-rays. Later, the x-ray technician arrived and asked the nurse (a different one), if he could move the baby. She told him "yes" without ever moving her eyes from the computer screen, which had also held her attention when the previous nurse had clearly told her the baby had been placed exactly as the doctor wanted it for the specific x-rays.

I moved so the machine could be placed between the incubators. Surprisingly, no lead apron or cover of any kind of was placed over the adjacent incubator, inches away. Later, the doctor would return, angry the baby had been moved.

"These x-rays are worthless, shoot them again. What happened to the nurse that was here?"

"She left," said the nurse still on the computer.

"Didn't she tell you how I wanted the baby? I gave her very detailed instructions," the frustrated doctor asked.

"No."

The nurse either lied or simply did not pay attention to the departing nurse. I had heard the previous nurse do her best to tell this nurse how the doctor wanted the baby placed, so the remaining nurse knew what to do.

Repeating herself, "She did not seem to understand the computer or was busy with it," the current nurse said.

"Pretty ironic," I thought.

"There are going to be more problems, more mistakes. There have been several this week; everyone trying to figure out the computer. This is a LOUSY time to be a patient," the doctor spat out.

Later, I would move, as the technician returned to shoot more x-rays, no cover to protect the three and a half-pound baby adjacent this time either. The saddest part, for me, was when the baby was ordered to surgery to cut his spine. From seeing the x-rays hanging on the wall and listening to the doctor, I knew he planned to operate on something I had seen change in babies with only one simple treatment. Even in adults, though it took a few treatments instead of one, tailbones had straightened out without surgery. It is so sad that there is not currently more complimentary care being utilized in conjunction with traditional medicine.

This was an excellent children's hospital. It is top of the line and many, many mommas and babies are helped. God Bless that staff. Lives are saved daily and they do all they can. If only they could do what they do, and other therapies could be added, so that even more could be done. That is my wish for the children of the world.

I had read of the frustration among hospital staff with computer time taking away from patient time. This incident was simply a graphic demonstration. Later, I would be with the mama of the baby that I was treating and another mama, whose baby had been resuscitated the day before, when he turned blue while she was holding him. The mama was understandably nervous. I had met her earlier in the Ronald McDonald room. It was my second day. The infant I was treating had gained a pound over the previous 24- hours and was off oxygen. I was still worried about him, but would have to fly back home at 6:00 a.m. the following morning, returning in five days.

Suddenly, the monitor next to us flat lined. The infant's mother looked to the mother I was with, who turned and looked at me. In a room with 20 babies that had been filled with doctors, nurses, and technicians all the time, there was no one except the two mamas, a room full of babies, and me. My feet were frozen next to the incubator while I looked in every direction for someone—anyone. Both mamas looked again at the flat lines still on the monitor, no heartbeat, no breath. They looked at me.

Mama said softly, "Is the baby dead?"

I could not touch any baby except the one I was there to see. NO one was in sight and I was not about to leave the baby to find someone. "Shake the baby," I told the mama.

She did. Nothing.

"Okay, shake the baby a bit more and make sure the wires are attached. Maybe they just came loose."

I could not touch the baby, but energy work can be done without physical touch, so I felt I was not breaking the rules now. A blip went across the monitor and then nothing. I increased the output of energy; last chance before we ran for anyone else to help.

"Shake the baby," I said softly, merging myself with the mama who could touch the baby.

Finally, a few more blips and then the monitor lines again came to life. Time seemed to have stopped, but mere seconds had passed.

"Shake the BABY?" my friends would say later, incredulous. "That was the best that you could come up with?"

"That's what the nurses would do; I watched them," I replied, aware that much more had happened than shaking the baby.

After four hours of sleep, I returned to the hospital at 4:00 a.m. to check on the baby then rushed to catch my plane. I still had a boatful of people going out at 7:30 a.m. on Maui. My husband noticed my stress when I snapped at him for approaching the whales too fast.

"What is up with you?" My husband asked with a puzzled look.

Then the dolphins surrounded our boat—ones we knew and had swum with regularly, but they were far from their usual spot.

"Come," they told me. "We have something special to show you,"

I knew they would help me relax after the hospital, so I went smoothly over the side of the boat into the incredibly soft aqua ocean. The dolphins brought leaves and bags to play catch, and chattered away. The females talk three times as much as the males, so maybe they are more like us than some folks believe. Then they swam me right up to a baby whale. Immediately, I surfaced and swam back to the boat.

"You know I cannot swim with whales, silly dolphins."

"You needed it after your trip to Oahu" they telepathed.

We moved away from the whale, and the dolphins followed. After about a quarter mile, they enticed me in again. Laughing and loving them, relaxed now, I swam for quite awhile. Suddenly, right behind me in the middle of dolphins was the baby whale again. The dolphins had played one of their usual games, sneaking up behind to see how close they could get to me before I realized they were there. Since I could not swim up to the baby, they thought it okay, apparently, to bring the baby to me. I immediately swam back to the boat and climbed in.

5

Many whales had caught me by surprise in the past, coming up to look me directly in the face, but I always bolted back to the boat as soon as I saw them. It is okay for them to come right up and rub against the boat, even reaching in to touch my husband, Ty, this season. It is not okay for me to approach.

The third time around, I caught on to what the dolphins were doing and stayed in the boat. I let the dolphins play in the boat wake, turning in a circle with them. Now clear they could not trick me into staying in the water and swimming to the whale, they amused themselves by getting me to go in tighter and tighter circles. Eventually, I just kept the boat on one spot and turned it round and round.

"NOW what are you doing?" my husband laughed.

"Just playing with my babies, the dolphins" I said, smiling softly.

"Well you are certainly in a better mood," he returned softly.

The dolphin's work sends me into difficult, sometimes heartbreaking, situations, but they always replenish my spirit as well as my body and emotions. I flew back and returned to the hospital to see the baby five days later. He was out of the incubator and had gained another two pounds. I could hold him in my arms instead of reaching into the incubator holes. There was only this tiny preemie and one other baby in the room.

I sang to him softly as I treated him, told him stories of his older brother who would arrive soon. Born 8-weeks premature, weighing in at under 3-lbs, with Respiratory Disease Syndrome, his lungs felt like they had been melted into a single mass. He became another miracle baby. He went home with his mama only 2-weeks old. He would come see the whales, whose songs I sang to him as a baby, when he was 14 months old. As if they knew him, four across, giant humpbacks rose out of the water in front of us and headed straight to the boat. At the very last minute, they dove directly under the boat, singing beautiful songs as we watched them swim below us in the crystal clear ocean.

KISSING WHALES HEALING DOLPHINS

I will never forget the brilliant smile the older brother, now 3 years old, flashed me. I have never seen him happier. The beaming toddler knew the magic of the whales that touched his brother in the hospital, and then again this day, in the clear blue ocean.

CHAPTER 2
FELICE AND CHRISTINE

It's time," Lori, one of my students, screamed with electric excitement over the phone line. "I will pick you up in five minutes."

"Give me 15, I need a shower."

Lori slammed down the phone without answering. I had already started a pile of things I would need, while on the phone with Lori: water bottle, sweater for the upcountry coolness, camera to "document," Peanut butter crackers. It had been less than an hour since we finished today's prenatal clinic at Kam One Beach. Christine had actually begun light labor during treatment and we participated with her moving the baby into the birth canal. It was awesome. A 38-year-old, first-time mom, she was a stuntwoman, gymnast, and surfer, who moved very well in her body. We kept reminding her to wait until her midwife got back on the island to have the baby. Her face was pure bliss as she undulated between our arms in the warm Maui Ocean. The baby rolled visibly under Christine's wetsuit. We had treated several mamas who were due in the next couple of weeks and a few more who had delivered in the last month. Lots of new babies had been given their first ocean treatment today.

We were still high from the energy of the clinic earlier this morning when Lori's jeep came flying into my driveway. Wet from the ocean, now wet from the shower, I jumped in and strapped down for what would be a 90-minute ride up the mountain, if I had been driving. Lori was a wild woman all of the time. Today, she was bursting. The back road up the mountain was full of twists and turns, but she would make the trip in 45-minutes. We fly by late-blooming Jacaranda trees with their brilliant purple flowers. The air turns cooler, filling with the smell of eucalyptus. Faster and higher, we flew up the jagged turns in the road into heaven. The island laid spread out below our feet, Haleakula crater rising into the clouds still higher above us.

"Oprah just bought a ton of property here," Lori said suddenly, breaking the silence. "She bought whatever anyone in the area would sell her."

We made a sharp turn up the mountain.

"This is one of the few properties she did not get, although some of the families around here would not consider selling, of course. We are surrounded on all sides now by parcels she bought."

Casual talk of someone like Oprah buying up pieces of land on Maui, or your running into Arnold Swartzeneggar out for ice-cream, have about as much importance as mentioning the Wall-Mart opening. It is just generic conversation. Maui is still a small island, like small towns everywhere, even if it does have areas of mega sparkle. Now, inside a little slice of heaven, surrounded by one of Miss Oprah's many dynasties, we were about to welcome a new little angel. The sun was close to setting and already the sky all around us was blazing with pinks and oranges, reflecting off the ocean now far below. We had passed tiny stone houses, plucked out of the distant past and scattered along the winding road. Lori turned sharply to the left, into a huge grove of deep green avocado trees. The giant fruit was everywhere you could see—lunch.

Lori pulled the jeep off the road into the grass and jumped out, running for the wood cabin ahead of us. I followed, scooping a ripe avocado off the ground and peeling the skin with my fingers. A couple bites of the creamy buttery fruit would last me awhile. This was not the condos of Kihei or the mansions of Wailea with golf course lawns. It would be Lori's first birth;

Chris, a friend of hers from Montana, and his wife, Felice, from New Mexico, having their first baby in this slice of mountain heaven.

Felice had started down the mountain for an AquaCranial treatment this morning when she started her labor. For several years, I have been running free prenatal, postnatal, and children's clinics. Included in the package is home treatment within hours of birth for the baby. Straight Craniosacral Therapy has been shown to substantially reduce, or even eliminate, such things as ADD, ADHD, Autism, Down's syndrome, colic, failure to thrive symptoms, epilepsy, Cerebral Palsy, and other challenges, when done within the first 48-hours after birth.

In some cases, we do Craniosacral and AquaCranial treatments during delivery. The baby then receives its first treatment in the birthing tub, still attached to the umbilical cord. Decompression of bones, tissue, and membranes allows the mother to relax and the birth to flow more easily. Care is taken to keep mama from being too relaxed, however, so that she continues to push. More and more midwives have come to us, interested in knowing how to incorporate AquaCranial Therapy into the birth process. Not only are births easier, recovery can be substantially faster.

Some of the midwives on Maui have their girls begin AquaCranial treatments as soon as they call looking for a midwife. We generally give 3 to 6 treatments to the mama in the last trimester. These make it easier for the mama to breathe, give the baby more space to move around, and relieve the mother's back pain and swelling. If the mother's pelvis is at all out of alignment, the pelvis is very gently realigned, which makes the actual delivery of the baby much easier.

Birthing assistance is available. Mamas receive postnatal treatments, usually two, when cleared by their doctor or midwife to get into the ocean. Babies usually receive two or three treatments within six weeks of birth and another two or three treatments the first year, if they are on the island. Many leave after the first month or two to return to the mainland, Europe, or wherever home is located. Some Japanese women come here to have babies that will then have duo citizenship. Other parents simply want their baby born in Hawaii, for a variety of reasons. About one-third of the mamas who come to us have a midwife, one-third are seeing a doctor, and one-third see both doctor and midwife. Usually the doctor is unaware of the midwife in the latter case. Some states, like Texas, pay for midwives with insurance, so more women see midwives there.

Thirty years ago I happened to be in the maternity ward of a large hospital when a new baby was brought from delivery to the nursery. The woman carrying the baby had obviously done her job so many times she could do it with her eyes closed. She was having a lively conversation with a nurse adjusting equipment in the nursery. Without even looking at the tiny naked baby she carried in one hand, she turned the dials of a giant silver fountain, shaped like the handle of a cane. With water blasting from the faucet, the woman never took her eyes off the nurse she was still conversing with as she mechanically stuck the minutes-old infant under the force of the water. I was shocked as I watched helpless through the glass window at the newborn suddenly twisting wildly, eyes wide open. The attendant shut off the water and wiped down the baby as she finished her conversation. She expertly and quickly wrapped the baby in a blanket then dropped it into a crib. She barely looked at the child. She never once uttered a word to it. I never forgot that baby's entry into the world and pledged to help change things. I have seen many wonderful hospital births. In La Jolla, California Scripp's Hospital has a birthing area with suites, music, water tubs, family is welcome—and all with complete hospital facilities down the hall. Still, that initial experience influenced my future work with pediatrics. My first conscious birth experience came years later.

I had been approached by people who were working with dolphins and the person who had pioneered underwater birth. The dolphins, they told me, wanted to work with me. At the time, talking to fish seemed rather insane to me, but my friend,

Grace, was into some wild stuff. She had "channeled" (I told you she was into wild stuff and this was in the Shirley McClain days) that many babies and children would one day come to Hawaii to see me and be healed. I did not even live in Hawaii at the time. The children would literally bring their parents. Eventually, what I began in Hawaii would grow there and expand to other places, with me traveling around the world to help children. So, Grace volunteered to let me begin my work with her yet unborn son, Mason. He was the first Conscious Birth experiment.

A decade later, I would start the Cetacea Bleu clinics. Nearly two decades later, I would be in the middle of Oprah's slice of heaven on the mountain, participating in the entry into this world of Hunter Dillon. His daddy had planned on a hospital birth, no ifs, ands, or buts, about it. When his wife wanted a midwife and he learned more, he was equally adamant about a home birth. Felice would wake-up to drive down the mountain at 5:30 a.m. for a sunrise AquaCranial treatment in the ocean far below. She came many times, wanting to do everything she could for her coming child. The two of them brought their baby into the world in the radiant glow of candlelight, surrounded by family and friends. Hunter rested on the soft waves made by his mama's breathing in the birthing tub, with a half a dozen hands touching him oh-so-gently, with unimaginable love; his daddy, his mama, grandma, grandpa, aunty, the midwives, and me.

Lori almost fainted at one point, not sure if she should run away or somehow save Felice. When she looked me in the eyes, she almost screamed out, "Is this normal? Is Felice okay?"

"It's cool" my eyes assured her. "They are doing great."

I smiled gently at Lori and she visibly relaxed. Having a baby is pretty physical. I highly recommend mamas prepare for birth as if they are preparing for a marathon run. Endurance, strong stomach muscles, and well-stretched, flexible thighs with plenty of strength, are necessary; walk, swim, do prenatal yoga. Felice recognized me when I walked in the door. At this point in labor, most mamas are not exactly conversational. I began decompressing her thighs between contractions. She smiled a tired, somewhat shocked smile.

"Hi Rebecca, glad you are here."

I stepped back as the midwives moved forward with the start of a new contraction; a dance we would do until after the birth. When Felice's face relaxed with the fading of the contraction, I once again switched places silently with the midwives. These women are incredible. Felice moved the baby into the birth canal with great effort, yet still like a pro. I was amazed to watch the physiological difference with Felice doing this squatting on dry land. It had been so much easier for Christine, the other mother I treated earlier the same day, to move her baby down into the birth canal while in the ocean.

You would have thought Chris, the hunter, fisherman, father, did this everyday. Sitting on the edge of the tub behind Felice, his arms under hers, he was magnificent. He seemed so capable, beyond his twenty-some years, somehow. The midwife put the heart Monitor on mama's tummy. Squeals and squeaks came out of the speaker along with the baby's heartbeat. Everyone in the room cracked up and laughed, "The dolphins are here."

Grandpa grabbed the flashlight when the midwife asked for one and found himself the keeper of the light.

"Shine it right in there, they told me," he would relate later.

I remember him peering over my shoulder, while I treated the baby in the tub, with a video camera. He was pretty comfortable in the middle of it all by then. When mama was on the bed, the midwives finishing their tasks with her, I laid the wrapped infant on the bed, off to the side and below mom's feet. Grandpa began touching baby's head oh-so-gently, doing some kind of energy work.

"Do you mind?" I asked as I gently began doing Craniosacral Therapy on Hunter Dillion's feet.

"Of course not. Feel the love," Grandpa said beaming.

13

Moments later, we wordlessly switched places. Grand-mamma was close.

"Put your finger lightly on the baby's heart," I asked her.

As soon as she did, the three of us connected to the baby and the room shifted. All at once, everyone, even those not looking, sucked in their breaths audibly and then breathed out "Awesome."

It was a baby born into a family full of love. It was perfect. It is not the only way for a perfect birth, of course. Babies come in many ways. Some hospitals have birthing rooms with tubs. Not everyone wants to have their baby at home, or perhaps they do not want anyone but the father and mother present. Other women do it completely on their own in a variety of circumstances. All the conscious love possible, whether by the parent, parents, or multiple friends and family—welcoming the new baby into this world with love is what makes a difference for the rest of a baby's life.

Christina's baby came soon after Felice had Hunter Dillion. I went alone this time. When I walked into the room, Christina was right there in the tub. She was very present when she looked me in the eyes. She smiled and made a grateful comment. I could tell she was completely exhausted, even though she would never complain. Her husband was holding the flashlight, standing at her feet. The midwife and her assistant were on either side of the tub.

"Jump on in, Rebecca," said the midwife who had done a birth with me before.

I stood behind Christina and touched her. No push left in this girl. When I slid my arms under hers and she grasped my hands and began pushing, she gave me a weak smile. I could see immediately that she was in trouble.

"Help me," she whispered softly.

When the next contraction began, my spirit slid into her body with her, physically pushing. Now it was going to move along. A couple of months later, Christine would talk about this moment.

"I could feel you move into my body and help me push, give me strength," she said. "That is the way it used to be. The women would gather and spiritually join with the mother to give her physical strength."

As soon as she said it, the sense of it was pretty obvious to me. When Ipo popped his head out after hours of pushing, everyone told Christine it would be easy now. Wrong. What a large chest he has. The second he is out, his eyes search out his mother's. He is sure that she is his first soul contact. Immediately, he then seeks out the midwife's face.

"What next?" his serious eyes ask hers.

He obviously knows she is the one who has coached him out the tunnel. After a moment of mamma bonding, the midwife holds Ipo on his back by his head. She does this with all the babies in the water so that the "natural swimming instinct" will kick in. The tiny baby begins moving his arms and legs in a natural backstroke.

"He is all yours," the midwife says, as she passes Ipo to me. Still attached to his mother's umbilical cord, Ipo has his first AquaCranial treatment. After a bit of time with Papa, I take Ipo, while his dad calls the family to spread the news of this special arrival. The midwife has mentioned a hematoma forming, so that is the first place I give Ipo attention. I then check out everything else and hand him to Mama. I treat her as we chat. Soon the midwife comes in.

"Oh, it is so hot in here. Mama and baby are sweating. Usually they are cool now." Suddenly a confused look crosses the midwife's face.

"I thought he had a hematoma, but I cannot find any signs of that now."

I leave quietly, while the midwife finishes her work. Later, Ipo will come with his family to the bay where a monk seal comes right up to him in the arms of his Hawaiian papa. Christine tells me that although she had breast reduction surgery, she has begun to nurse Ipo, against great odds. She is sure it was the AquaCranial prenatal treatments. I am equally sure it was

15

REBECCA GOFF

her determination and hard work. She wore a harness around her neck which held a container for milk with tubes that hung down and then attached to her nipples. .Other mamas had donated fresh breast milk. Even the midwife had told her to use formula—the risk of aids and other disease too great.

Christina had turned to Robin, another midwife and Maui angel, to find suitable, healthy milk for her baby. Ipo had milk from women from all around the world: Yugoslavia, Germany, Hawaii, Japan, and more—truly a special baby.

Weeks later Felice brought Hunter Dillion to the clinic for her postnatal treatment and his first ocean treatment. We bring in very special swim trainers from Germany, the best equipment for flotation I have ever found. Many were donated by the famous photographer Dimitri Lerner and his beautiful wife, Stephanie, from Germany. Hunter loves his and has been going in the water with his mama regularly. She is so dedicated and loves that boy. More than any mother, she brings him to swim and get his AquaCranial treatments, driving over an hour each way. He was only five months old when he first swam with dolphins.

I had finally gotten brave enough to take Mamas by myself, if the conditions were absolutely perfect; glass clear water all the way to the sandy bottom, all reefs completely visible, mirror flat water, no wind, and I mean absolutely, Nada—of course, willing dolphins and mamas who could swim well.

Felice arrived on one of those days. Her mother, Kata, had taken AquaCranial training and attempted to swim with dolphins in the past with no luck. She was here today with Felice and Hunter.

"Do you want to take Hunter Dillion out to the dolphins with me? The kayak is set up. The dolphins are here. I just came back in from swimming with them. Your mom can swim beside us. All you have to do is sit in the boat and hold Hunter Dillion; I will paddle. The boat is a two-man, and I have lifejackets and snorkel gear for you and everything. Would you be

16

okay if the boat tipped and you had to hold on to Hunter Dillion?" I asked Felice.

Even though she looked a bit nervous, she agreed to go. It was only minutes to get out to the dolphins across the beautiful blue water. We put Hunter in his swimmer, strapped the harness tight and Felice put him in the water with me. Several dolphins swam right up. Some came within inches of Hunter; dolphin faces out of the water, nose to nose with him—dolphin and 5-month-old baby, looking each other in the eyes.

Other people swam up to us, as that is where the dolphins were playing.

"Hey it's Hunter and Felice," sang out a volunteer therapist who knew them from the clinics. "Without your mask, you cannot see the dolphins under you. They are obviously way more active under you and the baby," she told us.

Felice stayed close to us and played with Hunter. She also had a few minutes to swim with the dolphins on her own. Hunter Dillion slid as far into his swimmy as possible and turned his head so his ear was in the water. An incredible look of joy spread over his face as the dolphins began making sounds wildly below him. Hunter smiled and began making sounds and laughing. For weeks after, even tourists who had been in the bay that day, talked of how the dolphins kept surrounding our kayak as I took out the babies, one after the other.

CHAPTER 3
JAYE

G od sent me Jaye, no doubt about it. She is such a sweetie. She would say it is the other way around, but do not believe it. I received phone calls and email from her. She recently moved to Maui and read about me in Massage Magazine. It was a great article, four pages, and awesome photos. I had already received calls from several teachers of other institutes who wanted to work for me. Who could blame them? The article had show cased therapists that I had trained at the Maui Four Seasons, where AquaCranial Therapy is on the menu. My therapeutic experiences with dolphins, whales, and babies, in the incredible Maui waters, had also been featured in the magazine article.

Jaye, a therapist, was asking just to speak with me for a moment. Luck was with her. There was a Basic Training for therapists starting almost immediately. She jumped for it.

We did not meet before the training. Everyone shows up for class on lava rocks. No walls, no audio/video equipment. There is only a bucket for a bathroom. Everyone is told we will be far from anything, and to bring water, snacks, and snorkel equipment. While the students were saying their hellos, getting their things arranged around their beach chairs on that first day, the dolphins arrived.

"Everyone have their snorkel, mask and fins?' I asked.

Lot's of nodding heads; an "of course" or two.

"Great," I tell them. "Get your gear, put on your wetsuits, and let's boogey. The dolphins are here now."

"You want us to go now?" Jaye asked somewhat incredulous.

"This is why you are here, sweetie. Let's go," I say, while grabbing my own gear.

Jaye takes her brand new, never-before before-used snorkel and mask out of their package with a look of "I don't know."

"It will be okay," I tell them. "Everyone pick a swimming buddy."

I quickly match up participants according to ability and experience. "Just remember, no hurries in or out. Relax and take it easy. Let's all swim out together in a group, okay?" I say while leading them to the ocean.

Then, they take that big leap. Step into the ocean and just swim out. This takes a great deal of courage for some. The kind of courage it will take their clients to go into the ocean for AquaCranial treatments later. What a start for fifty-year-old Jaye who had never snorkeled before in her life!

The dolphins whizzed by everyone, but the water was not too clear, so most did not see them. The dolphins zapped everyone with their energy, but did not stay close to play. It was thrilling to most students to just to make that jump into the big, wild, ocean.

It was always going to be the big steps for Miss Jaye with me. She took the beginning training—four days. She signed on for the 300-hour certification at that point. Already very well trained in Craniosacral Therapy, it was the water therapy she came to learn from me. I set an appointment to have her kayak with me. It was also her first time in a kayak.

When we arrived at the bay, the ocean was like suds in a washing machine—very turbulent. We launch out over sharp, black, lava rocks. Big waves were breaking on shore in front of us. As I held onto the front of the kayak, which was bouncing on the waves, I looked at her.

"Sure you are up for this?"

"I do not know," Jaye answered. "But I want to get to the dolphins and they are just right on the other side of the big waves, so let's do it."

"Good girl. Come on up and climb into the front seat here in the boat."

Just as Jaye got settled in, the "BIG WAVES" started. Something everyone should know about the ocean is that the waves come in sets. Every eight sets or so, the waves get much bigger. So, you can be prepared for 2-foot waves and suddenly they are 4 or 5-feet high. I knew I was going to get knocked down if I was going to hang on to the kayak, which I had to do, because Jaye was already in it. The tide was up, so I could see the easiest thing to do was to go down and ride the waves into the beach, holding tight to the kayak to keep it upright. I did not want it to flip and throw Jaye onto the rocks her first time out. So, that is what I did.

The first wave hit me and knocked me down, but it was not a big deal, as I was already prepared to ride it, which I was doing quite successfully. When we went a few feet out of the break line, I jumped up and said, "Okay, let's paddle out now."

"Are you okay?" Jaye asked with a horrified look on her face.

"Fine," I said. "Just get ready to paddle."

I really was okay, but I knew it had to be something of a shock for Jaye, as she would tell people later. All she saw was the waves knock me down and the kayak drag me, seemingly, across the sharp rocks, while she watched helplessly, sitting calmly and perfectly in the kayak—which did not flip. She could not believe it when I jumped up and said I was fine.

"But, you were fine," she would say with amazement later.

We paddled on out with no further incidence. Once we were out about a quarter mile, I told Jaye to put on her gear. The dolphins were heading our way.

"Where are they?" she asked.

"Look about 20-feet in front of your kayak. Pretend the kayak is a clock with the front being twelve. The dolphins are at about two on the clock."

"Oh my! They ARE right there," she exclaimed.

"Here they come," I told her, as they made a slight turn and

20

headed directly for the kayak.

In minutes, they surrounded our kayak.

"Oh no, I missed them," Jaye cried out as the dolphins swam off.

I laughed. "Just get in the water, Jaye. They will come back. They are in play mode." I slipped into the silky blue water.

"Wow, the boat did not even move. How did you do that?" Jaye asked.

"Just slide in gently. Don't worry about the boat. I pull it around with me by the leash."

Jaye slid into the water. I silently began communicating with the dolphins. "This is Jaye," I told them. "She has come to help me with the babies and learn what you have taught me. Want to give her the big welcome?" I asked.

Almost immediately, Jaye was surrounded by dolphins—nearly sixty of them.

"Oh, my gosh," she gasped.

"Remember the rules. Look for the boat to find me. Have fun."

Jaye swam with them a bit then returned to me. "I can't quite see them now," she said.

There were two dolphins about a foot behind her.

"Come with me," I told her, taking her hand.

The dolphins surrounded us on all sides and below us. We swam with each other and the dolphins for a couple of hours that day. Finally, it was time to go back in. Of course, I had to actually convince Jaye to get back in the boat!

"Time to go" I said. "The winds are kicking up and the waves are even bigger than when we came out, so we need to get back in. Get in the boat and take off your fins. You will need your reef shoes back on land on the rocks."

"Okay, HOW do I get in the boat?" she asked.

"There are fancier ways, but I just throw myself across the boat like a beached whale and go from there. It helps if you kick hard a few times then propel yourself up into the boat."

Jaye was pleasantly surprised at how easily she managed.

"You are a natural," I laughed.

It had only been a moment since I had told Jaye to jump in the boat when the winds turned wicked.

"How did you know the wind was going to do this?" Jaye asked.

"I see it coming on the water and try to stay ahead of it. You can be blown to sea in minutes with an offshore wind. Take a ride on the Tahiti Express."

I was referring to the currents right out of the bay. The wind was blowing harder now; you could see whitecaps.

"Okay Jaye, we are going to land where we launched."

Jaye looked at the waves we had to paddle through now, which were three or four times higher then when we launched.

"We cannot do this," she said suddenly panicked.

"No problem," I told her.

She was really scared and going into a kind of shocked trance.

"Can't do, Can't do it," She repeated.

The winds were actually howling now. I shouted above the sound.

"Watch the wave. Look at it. It is breaking big to the left, but it gets smaller and smaller to the right. We will land at the very small end. It is easy; you just surf in on the waves. Watch the boat in front of us."

About a moment later, that boat flipped over.

"Okay, not that way," I laughed. "The reef and current there will suck us into the cliffs if we are not careful, so we are going to shoot for a specific spot. You just paddle steady and strong. I will guide us in. Easy."

I had just about convinced Jaye. She was relaxing somewhat. It was a challenge, but now everything was under control and I had a plan. We could make it with a bit of work.

"Help me," a girl called. She was flailing in the water about 15-feet away from us.

I looked over as another wave threw her under.

"You have to help me," she screamed as she went under. There was sheer panic in her eyes when she surfaced again.

In that moment, I felt like I knew what people must have felt in situations like the Titanic. I could get myself and Jaye in, but there was no way I could even try to get a third person through without the very real possibility of Jaye and me not making it in the effort. The girl in the water had fear and panic in her eyes as they locked on the kayak. I knew if she tried to climb on—what she saw as her only salvation—the boat would swamp and we would all be in trouble. I tried talking to her to calm her.

"What is wrong?"

She was about 10-feet from the boat now. I was trying to keep it steady and get closer to her. Die or not, we had to try to help her. We were in an area that was very volatile, waves hitting from three directions, currents and wind trying to smash us into the jutting edges of the cliff, or throw us onto the hard rocks, which were full of razor sharp corals, and crush us with the giant waves crashing down on us. You would not normally try to "sit still" here; you would shoot through the channel and get out of the trouble zone. This was not an option today.

"I keep getting slammed by the waves, I need to get oriented, I cannot find the shore," the girl shouted before being dragged to the bottom once again.

"Grab the lifejacket on the front of the boat and give it to me," I shouted at Jaye, above the wind.

This time, I was right next to the unknown woman when she surfaced.

"Put your arms through the holes in this lifejacket. Lay on it like a float."

We were dragging her by her bathing suit, inch by inch, out of the danger zone as she put the jacket on. Almost instantly, she relaxed. I have people lay on the jacket because the feeling of support under their stomach and chest gives them the feeling that they are landing on something solid after the constant movement of the ocean, and it is immediately comforting.

"You are okay, just relax and stay next to us. You cannot get in the boat, but we will not leave you."

The panic was settling. We had given the unknown woman a rope to hold onto, and together we were getting out of the trouble spot and closer to land.

"Breathe, Jaye," I told her. "Paddle strong."

We were quite close now.

"We are going into the side bay. Only land here in emergencies, but this counts."

My husband had arrived and was making his way out across the reef to meet us. "Help her," I called to him, pointing at the woman attached to our boat.

He nodded and headed out to us.

"Look, look up. See the cute guy with the long hair? He is coming to help you."

She looked at me and smiled, even though you could see she was exhausted. "Thanks, you saved me. I was fine, and all of a sudden, the wind and waves went nuts. I can swim now." She was ready to cry.

"You are okay now," I said softly.

We made it to the calmer water of the Baby Bay and Ty was almost to her.

"Come this way," he called, reaching out to her.

She swam towards him, and he towards her, and then he helped her to very unsteady feet. You always have to be aware of the power of nature and her ability to shift in a moment. Jaye and I cruised lightly onto the reef.

"Way to go, Jaye!"

She was laughing now.

"How about a nice easy day of home visits tomorrow?" I asked her.

"Sounds great to me," she said, and we made plans for the next day while stripping down the kayak and loading it on to my truck.

Jaye said she slept for hours that afternoon. She was very brave. 7:00 a.m. the next morning, we met at Jamba Juice where Jaye would leave her car. She had not been on the island long and had not been to many places. Our first stop was more than an hour away—straight up the mountain from the desert where we live, but there is no road straight up. The whole thing was owned by the Ranch, and no one up there wanted all the tourists to be able to shoot straight into the neighborhood.

It was very tranquil up the mountain; nothing like the crowded streets and backed-up traffic in Kihei—and even Wailea and Makena these days. So, we drove to the center of the island, the industrial area where the airport was located. Only recently, have Costco and Wal-Mart come to our island, located on the way out to the airport, for the convenience of tourists.

From there, we drove up the mountain, and then back south another half an hour. In the mountains, there is open land, lots of cactus and rolling pastures. The rocks go from small to huge boulder sizes; sometimes the land is nearly barren and then it changes, and it is so covered with rocks that you can barely see land. Everywhere, cactus springs out of the ground, looking so unlikely that it seems surreal. A low hanging mist often hovers over the ground. It is very quiet. Looking down at the little specks so far below, you feel like you are looking at monopoly buildings instead of the sprawling giants that are called resorts. Their world famous pools are not even visible, and the ocean seems like it goes on forever in front of the gold coast beaches.

We passed the now-famous "Oprah" land, and drove past the labyrinth so many walked during years of full moons. Other landmarks: the only store—best pastries in the world. You could drive 20-minutes or more and see no one, unlike driving two blocks in 20-minutes of crawling traffic amidst hundreds of people along the coast below. The trip was just miles of scenic and uncluttered driving straight down the mountain. No wonder the mountain people want to keep the peace that is there.

"It is worth the extra drive," I always think when I come up here.

The air is so fresh. Very different from the vog, dust, or worst of all—the cane smoke that we have down below.

"Here it is, the Sun Yat Sen Park," I announced.

In the middle of what appeared to be a rocky cow pasture, on a slope down the side of the mountain, was a large sculpture of a man. I remember the first time we happened by here and I wondered, "What the heck is that?"

Later, I discovered the statue was of a man who was exiled here from China; a great revolutionary.

"Okay, park next left up the hill, second road back."

We turned up a road, unlike Jaye had ever seen on the East Coast, judging from the look on her face, as the gears ground on the steep incline. I bounced around the deep ruts where the road had washed out. Seeing a man working on the side of the road, I pulled up close and rolled the window down further.

"Aloha. Do you know Mark and Sally? Just had a new baby a couple of days ago?"

"Not here. Maybe up the hill. Want to use my cell phone?"

"I have a cell phone," Jaye suddenly announced.

"Good apprentice. I threw mine away after I left the Four Seasons. One phone and email is more than enough for me."

Jaye loved working with the tiny newborn; this one a bit colicky. I can tell what is upsetting a baby's tummy, and many times track it to what the mama was eating when she was nursing. Usually, eliminating the offending food eliminates the baby's tummy ache. Once, I tracked it to the coconut milk in the curries one mother was eating the day before her delivery.

Down the hill to the next house we go, in a neighborhood with signs and paved streets. We are on our way to a healthy, happy, newborn. It was looking easy now.

Next baby is way out into the jungle. We approached a road that looked pretty scary, to put it mildly.

"I don't know. I am not sure this is it."

The road was really shaky and the neighborhood was known for renegade drug makers. If I had known this was it, I would have tried, but… this was tricky.

"Hey, let's call," I said, remembering Jaye's cell phone.

When there was no answer, I decided that I would try again in a couple of days, but this time, I would bring my husband with me. He was much braver driving certain roads than I am.

You could tell Jaye was visibly relieved, even before she said, "Great idea; come back with Ty."

"Okay, only one baby to go today," I tell Jaye.

We had driven four hours already, and had covered several areas of the island—all new terrain to Jaye.

"Remember the twin falls. Then the next left where the big rock is painted blue." We were following island style directions.

Down to the bottom of the hill, then I pull off on the side of the road. There is a path leading up somewhere into the jungle.

"This is it," I say, opening my door.

Jaye looks dubiously up the muddy path leading into nowhere.

"Are you sure?" she asks.

I look at my paper taped to the dashboard with all the directions and notes for today's mamas and babies.

"Twin falls, blue rock left, second right, third path into jungle, past second house. Yes, this is it. Let's go."

Jaye takes a deep breath and starts up the path. The woman we are going to see has not let anyone near her or the baby, except a midwife in the neighborhood who showed up after the mama had pushed for hours trying unsuccessfully to deliver alone. The midwife, who had called me to come, said she did not think the baby would have made it had she not shown up. This was a week ago; the baby now seven days old.

The mama had refused to see anyone. Her pregnancy had a lot of drama. It seems the mother was devastated when the baby's father abandoned her late in the pregnancy. She had moved many times in that month and a half before ending up in this jungle tree house. While it could have been ideal under some conditions, it was very cold, damp, and isolated right now. She felt she had been abandoned by the world and had pretty much given up. Her baby, lying in the same bed beside her, also felt abandoned. Emotionally, his mother was not there. He was lying in his own waste when we arrived.

I felt like walking straight out the door with him in my arms. Instead, I said, "Hi, I am Rebecca. I am going to help your son, and Jaye is going to help you," very matter-of-factly. "Just lay across the bed with your head here so that Jaye can get to you easier."

She stared at me for a minute, and then simply said, "Okay."

She lay as I asked, then closed her eyes again. I picked up the baby, cleaned him up and changed him into fresh clothes. Jaye and I silently went to work. It had been fun and laughter and lighthearted work with babies earlier today. This was more serious, and we both knew it without speaking. When I had first picked the baby up, he looked me deep in the eyes, then just looked away and checked out, without even closing his eyes. This concerned me more than his physical health; this emotional withdrawal. I knew this one was in for trouble if we did not help him quickly. He slept deeply after we left, as did his mama. I would go back the next day, bringing warm clothes and blankets for both mama and baby. I wanted to check on her right away. I was concerned for the baby's welfare, yet I still wanted to give the mama a chance to get on her feet physically and emotionally.

Leaving the children with their mother is best, if the mother can care for them. When I returned, she was up and dressed, and both she and the baby looked immensely better. She really looked at me for the first time when I was handing her the things I had brought.

"WHO ARE YOU?" she asked. "I am so grateful, wherever you came from. I felt I had been completely deserted, nobody cared, and I was so cold. Someone even showed up today with a heater and put plastic over the windows."

She was a new person. Later, she would move into a warm house, her mom would come visit, and slowly but surely, the baby would get over his anger at their early time together. At first, he would scream for hours. His mama would look at me deeply with her wise eyes, "He is very angry at me," she would say softly.

Every time I took him away from his mom, he would fall soundly asleep in my arms. I would carry him until his sleep was so deep that he would not wake up when I laid him down. I was able to get him into the kayak and out with the dolphins the same flat, perfect day Hunter Dillion had his first dolphin swim. It was his mama I wanted swimming with dolphins, and she did. A very articulate, well-educated young woman, she pulled herself out of the depths of despair, laughing while slipping and sliding through the waves, just like the dolphins who played with her.

I made a pad with the life jacket on the kayak in front of me, covered it with a towel, and placed the tiny, seven-week-old infant on top. I gave him his treatment while the dolphins surrounded us and adjusted his electrical field. He and mama are doing better all the time. The bad memory of the first time we met faded away eventually. It was very sobering for Jaye.

"Well your life is not just about the Four Season's kinds of resorts and treating movie stars. This is serious stuff."

She was amazed when I told her of my subsequent visit to the mama and that she was up and about.

"YOU are KIDDING!" She said. "No, you are amazing."

"It was you that worked on that mama, Jaye. Sometimes, a little bit can change a lot. By the way, I have a private client staying at the Seasons. Would you like to help me treat him tomorrow? He is a cool guy who teaches 40 some workshops a year and is internationally known for his sports medicine work."

"Really, I can assist you at the Four Seasons? YES!"

After the hour and a half ride home, Jaye went to sleep. We met the next morning on the beach in front of the Seasons. The beach boy set up our chairs as we got on our wetsuits. One of the Season's therapists I trained had been booked with an ocean

AquaCranial Therapy session and was setting up his chairs.

"Cool," he said when he saw me. "Big waves today," he laughed.

This would be Jaye's first big wave treatment and she was eyeing the huge waves slamming on the beach.

"I love big waves," I laughed back.

The local boys who work at the beach thought I was crazy. The giant waves would crash, obliterating the view of us with the spray of white water. When the water settled, the client was still peacefully floating above it all. I could see the look, yet another one, in Jaye's eyes, as the wave lifted her six feet off the ocean floor. This was not just deep water; it was moving and crashing all around us. My client did deep-water treatments every year and loved it, so he was just floating calmly through it all.

"You were amazing. You just kept doing all this detailed work like he was on a table," She would tell me later.

"You will get there. It just takes practice."

Right now, she was doing her best not to swallow the entire ocean, so said nothing. Suddenly, a big wave broke over us. I looped my arms under my dreaming client and rode over the wave with him. It picked Jaye up, rolled her over a few times, and then spit her out on the beach. She tried to come back out twice, but could not get through the break. I just laughed when she threw her arms up in an "I give up" expression.

"Time to wake up," I told the client who opened much altered eyes. I helped him out of the ocean, motioned to Jaye to follow, and headed up to the pools.

We all slid into the large Jacuzzi. The fountain behind us spilled from some ten feet above into the pool below. Lying with his head in a pillow, the client allowed us to move him back and forth between us, coaxing the pain and tension out of his body. A fire burned in the large outdoor fireplace a few feet away. Paradise. Finally, we brought him out and took him to lay in the comfy lounge chair already covered with fresh towels.

"How about kayaking again tomorrow," I asked Jaye.

"Absolutely," she replied immediately.

This is the last peek into the life of an AquaCranial apprentice. We met the next morning as the sun was rising over the mountain. Pink light shot across the sky and seemed to fill the bay. I brought my two-year-old grandson. The dolphins had played in my heart on the way here, so I knew we would have an encounter.

"Beach, Grandma?" Jacob asked as we passed our usual beach.

"Beach way down there," I said pointing down the road.

Jacob was out with whales when he was four months old, but this would be his first dolphin encounter. He lives on Kauai with his mama and visits two or three times a year for a couple of weeks. He loves swimming in his red swimmy. Today was one of those completely perfect days; totally flat and glassy, no wind, and water you could almost walk on.

At this point, I had never paddled out a mama and child. I would be in a separate kayak; the mama and baby would be paddled out by Ty, her husband, or someone else strong and capable of handling the kayak. We usually went out four adults per child. Jacob was leaving tomorrow and something told me to go for it. This was Jaye's second time in a kayak.

"All you have to do is hold Jacob and make sure nothing happens to him if we flip over. I will do all the paddling."

Jaye looked like the last thing she wanted was to be responsible for the safety of MY grandbaby, but she kept looking over her shoulder at the dolphins playing close to shore. The dolphins won. We paddled out easily. Jacob was always pointing out dolphin art, dolphin photos, and dolphin wind chimes to me.

"Dolphin," he would say. I think it was one of his first words. Now he was chanting in the boat, "Dolphin, Dolphin."

We put him in his swimmy, heading further out into the ocean. Suddenly, Jacob River saw the dolphins.

"OH… DOLLLPHHINS!" he exclaimed, his eyes suddenly

wide. "Swimming, Grandma, swimming," he shouted as he tried to leap out of the boat.

I slid in and Jaye passed him to me.

"You have the boat," I smiled at her, swimming off with Jacob River.

He is very fast, so you have to really swim to keep up. There were three of the tiniest dolphins I have ever seen in the bay that day. They would leap and flop on the water all around Jacob River, over and over, while he squealed with delight. For over an hour the dolphins played with us. Jacob River got cold.

"Boat, Grandma."

When I tried to put him in the boat though, he would cry, "No, Grandma, swimming, swimming!"

Finally, I put him in the boat and wrapped him in my warm, dry, sweatshirt.

"Dolphins, Dolphins!" he called.

The dolphins seemed to come from all over the bay to our boat. They were leaping and spinning while Jacob River laughed and clapped. The dolphins swam away and Jacob began to cry.

"Again, dolphins, again," cried the two-year-old.

"That doesn't work," I tried to tell him, but before I could finish, the dolphins were once again coming from all directions to leap around our boat. Jacob River just laughed and clapped, jumping and squealing like a dolphin himself.

Several more times they would leave, only to return when Jacob River would cry out, "Again, dolphins, again."

It was unreal. I could feel that he had finally had enough; the energy is strong, so we headed to shore. The dolphins swam all the way in with us, right next to the kayak. They are so amazingly beautiful. As we turned in to land, we saw that the waves were up. Kayaks were rolling and flipping, one after another going in, even though the water was glassy. Jaye was nervous now.

"This is going to be cake," I told her. "See where everyone is trying to land is just at the end of the wave break, so it is rolling them over. We are going just about ten feet farther over to avoid the break."

Usually that would have crashed us on the higher rocks, but today, Mother Nature was with us. The tide was really high, and we floated easily over the top of the rocks and onto the beach.

"Perfect," Jaye said. "Although I knew it would be with your grandson in the boat."

"You are a pro now yourself," I responded. "You know, that is a first for me. You have given me confidence in my own abilities after all these years, to do more things without Ty. It is quite empowering. Mahalo."

I sent Jaye back out to swim with the dolphins awhile longer and put Jacob River in the truck for the ride home. He began to cry deeply.

"No, Grandma. Beach way back there—beach," he sobbed. After a few minutes, he stopped crying, took a deep breath and looked at me. "I'm okay now, Grandma," the little two-year-old said just plain as day, looking deeply into my eyes.

"You're okay now?" I repeated.

"Yes," he said simply. Then he slept for hours.

CHAPTER 4
ISLANDS OF CHRISTINA

S he was not my first client in the Cetacea Bleu program. Christina's immune system was destroying her nervous system. She lay curled in a fetal position, suffering indescribable pain before being diagnosed. Still not sure exactly what the problem was, Steroids, Chemo, and other drugs had been used to destroy or breakdown her immune system, so that it would no longer attack her nervous system. This actually helped, but was not a course of therapy that could be continued. The drugs can only be given for so long. That time was coming to an end for Christina. Her family contacted me a few months earlier. Make a Wish foundation had offered to send Christina to Sea World to see dolphins. Her family wanted a more natural environment and had heard of Cetacea Bleu and our cetacean assisted therapy. Her father told me he was not looking for a miracle or an answer to the problem (He was.). They simply wanted to give their daughter an experience to carry her through the needles, blood exchanges, and her dying body. He told me the nerves in her legs were dead. They had already spent half a million dollars on therapy and there was still no hope. I told them all I could offer was perhaps some relief from the trauma and a bit of soothing for her soul. Dad said that would be enough and they made the arrangements to come.

I have other stories of healing more dramatic, but not more meaningful for Christina's parents than her story. The treatment was more time intensive than usual for me, but necessary in this case. We had a short time, and every day Christina's body called me back for more, so together, we went for it.

The First Day: Christina and her family met us at a beach near their condo. Although not meeting my eyes for the first five minutes, Christina quickly warmed up to me and we played a bit in the sand. I did my initial evaluation and then touched on some points with the parents. Her pelvis had smashed in on itself repeatedly. This appeared to come from her constant falls. She fell every two or three steps at this point. Her parents were amazed at how well she took to me. While I have a lot of experience and a bit of a touch, I also bring presents. That first night, Christina gave me a present also. A rubber gecko she found in the sand... the middle of the deserted beach... in the dark. There was a general weakness in Christina's Craniosacral system with a specific weakness in her lungs. Her legs felt so light; it was as if they were totally empty, but with patience, they decompressed. Her Craniosacral rhythm strengthened and she relaxed noticeably.

Day Two: We again met at the beach in the evening. After this second treatment, her hips completely decompressed and literally felt stronger. The legs continued to decompress and continued to feel "empty—no weight." Her father continued to remind us that the nerves in the legs were dead.

Day Three: Christina was eager for our couple of hours at the beach. Her emotional state was changing for the better. As we explored the beach, discovering several "islands of Christina" and "islands of Rebecca," it was obvious her legs were working much better. She could walk for ten or more minutes without falling.

As the sun set, Christina piped up, "Look at the light on the water, it is so beautiful. And the rocks. Look! Just look at them. They are so lovely. This is so beautiful, Rebecca. I could do this every night. We are having quite the adventure, aren't we?"

You could no longer tell who loved whom more.

Day Four: We were at the bay. The dolphins were in; this is

why they had brought Christina. However, she would not even think about getting into the water! One drop on her and she had to have her clothes changed immediately, but she was willing to sit on the beach and watch me get into the water—which I do, fully dressed. Taking the opportunity when it arose, Christina allowed me to put her into a wet suit so I would not get her wet in my now-soaked clothes when I carried her. The whole family tried on wetsuits. A short treatment, then back to the condo to rest.

Day Five: Treatment at the beach. Christina was getting stronger and happier. No more weakness in her lungs. A strong flow in the Craniosacral system. We decide to try for dolphins tomorrow. The family remembers to tell me that the compression in her frontal bone that I have detected, and have been releasing, could have come from a fall she took shortly before her illness appeared. A large fluid bump had risen on her forehead at the time.

Day Six: On this day, I decided presents were not enough to get this girl in the water, so I had a family who had been with the Cetacea Bleu program for over a year join us at the bay. They had a daughter Christina's age and a son the same age as Christina's brother, Luka. Members of this family included Thomas, now 14 months old, who had been out in the kayaks close enough to touch whales when he was four months old. His sister Tracy, now four, was my way to get Christina into the water.

While Christina was still not ready to kayak, she did let me pull her all over the Baby Bay with Tracy in a small blow-up boat. Dad went out in the kayaks with the boys: Benjamin, now six and a pro at Cetacean kayak trips, his dad, a couple of visiting cousins with their dad, and of course, Ty. This was when therapy began to extend to the family. Ty mentioned to Christina's father, Steven that he may not want to continue to reinforce the idea to Christina that the nerves in her legs were dead. As mom, Nona, received her AquaCranial treatment and played with the other children and their mom, Becky, Steven remembered how to let go and enjoy the ocean. Steven is Christina's daddy. The dolphins did not come that day. Everyone was having such a good time that they did not notice. Nevertheless, you could see the miracle the ocean, the sunshine, and the peace of nature was reintroducing to this family on a quest for their daughter.

Day Seven: I am really bugging dad, Steven, now. He must have answered the same questions for me a dozen times. I am bugging other therapists for information, pulling out all my resource books and burning up the Internet. I see progress— improvements. I want to know as much as possible. I treat Christina on the couch in the condo as her parents watch.

"Well Christina, I must say you are getting stronger every day," I tell her.

She immediately looks at her parents with veiled eyes to see their reaction. Mom does her best, but cannot sound convincing. When I tell Christina she is my best patient ever, both parents enthusiastically agree and support her verbally. I casually mention that tomorrow we will kayak. Christina has seen everyone get ready, take off, and land. I remind her that the following day she will see Tracy again and will now be able to tell Tracy that she has kayaked too.

Day Eight: Christina is carried out and put in my lap on a VERY DRY towel. Her father is in the backseat of the kayak to paddle us. Brother Luka is put in his mamma's lap with Ty to kayak her. Did I mention as soon as the lifejacket and wetsuit went on Luka he began to scream? I always kayak myself, so I was learning to let go as well, holding Christina in my lap a few inches from the water. The water was so clear you could watch the bottom go further away from us. At first, we looked at the corals and where the sand patches appeared a brilliant blue from the water. When Christina began to get nervous, I pointed out the buoy a few hundred feet ahead of us and suggested we race. Two friends in one-man kayaks had joined our group this day.

Christina is aggressive and competitive, so she loved the

race idea. She reached out to touch the buoy, laughing joyfully. I realized at this point that her brother Luka had not quit screaming since we put him in the suit and lifejacket twenty minutes earlier. His mother is from Georgia, which was part of Russia until a decade ago. Somewhere, Luka had developed a very strong personality. Ty kayaked a disappointed mama and screaming baby back to shore, agreeing to drive the truck and meet us at a beach a couple of miles down.

Turtles came to the boat and raised their heads to look at us; Christina loved it. When many people hear music, they hear mostly the whole composition. A musician is much more likely to hear the individual instruments, the way the composition weaves mathematically, etc. It is a type of discernment. I feel things in the human bodies of others that have a physical presence and can be measured on instruments, but may be too subtle for most people to notice. When I work on children, they can feel their spines "grow." I can touch them, play with them, but the moment I engage their Craniosacral systems, they KNOW exactly what I am doing. They FEEL it. Adults feel the movement of their Craniosacral system about 50% of the time if it is pointed out to them, usually in their sacral area as it decompresses. Occasionally, an adult feels it clearly. If I have not explained earlier, I do Craniosacral Therapy (CST), and throw it in as part of a massage. Clients often tell me that it feels as if their body is magically growing.

Gymnasts usually have strong, flowing, systems that are easy for them to feel. People who do yoga have great systems, and when there is no emotional problems, most can easily feel the flow. I felt Christina's entire biology, "drop" and become "loose energy." The only other time I had experienced this particular "feeling" was when someone was receiving chemotherapy in the hospital. I later found out that Christina was taking a daily form of chemo. At this time, I only knew that her body was going through some kind of healing crisis. As she slumped in my lap on the kayak, all her strength seemingly sapped from her body, she asked to go back to the condo. We kayaked up to the beach where her mother, her now sleeping brother, Luka, (stopped crying the minute the lifejacket came off), and Ty waited for us. We felt both peace and sadness. The plan was to not see Christina or her family for a day, then to meet for a big boat trip.

Day Nine: No therapy today.

Day Ten: Christina's episode on day eight reminded me of how fragile she is. Instead of a half-day trip to Lanai, I opt for the two-hour whale watch on a big boat to get us into deep water. As the family walked up, I saw Christina looking at me with mistrust in her eyes. Her father explained that they had spent the previous day in the Maui hospital. Once again, Christina had needles put into her. Her energy had dropped and there was blood in her urine. Tests showed that the blood was only a side-effect of her medication, and that Christina was fine, according to the doctor.

Slowly, Christina opened up as we toured the boat and found seats. Ten minutes in and a whale breached right next to Christina, closer than 30-feet from the boat. Before it was back underwater, another whale breached right beside it. This whale breached in a side position, showing off his tummy. As all the people on the boat went wild, the crew announced we should just enjoy the ride, as it cannot get any better than the show we just had. While several other whales visited us that day, Christina and I were inside playing with the plastic whales that the crew had loaned us. The entire family relaxed more than ever as the whales played around the boat. Christina was beaming. She loved the trip, she told me, and it was so obviously true.

More presents as we go our separate ways for the day, and a promise to kayak tomorrow with dolphins and new friend, Tracy.

Day Eleven: The last day on Maui for the family is beautiful. The water is flat and velvety, the most perfect children's boat day. I literally feel the love coming from Ty's heart as he burst out loud; he hopes the dolphins will come. They do. They are waiting when we arrive. Becky is there with her three children at 7:00 in the morning; bless her. Ty takes Becky, 6-year-old Benjamin, and fourteen-month-old Thomas out in the kayak with him. As they blissfully watch the dolphins swimming around the kayak not far from shore, Tracy and I wait for Christina and her family on this perfect, perfect, day. Perfect, until I realize that I had not called to confirm which beach and the family was obviously not coming, as they were already 45-minutes late.

After trying to send "mental messages" to please come, Tracy and I climbed into my truck and drove off through the lava fields, trying to find the Sprint signal for my cell phone. A few minutes down the road, we found the family approaching. They had waited for my call, but decided to just find us, when it became obvious that I had blown it.

We all headed back to the dolphins. Becky, Ty, and the boys are just pulling up to shore in the kayak as we all arrive in our vehicles. Everyone is excited. As we decide who will ride with whom, the little girls get nervous and begin backing away, saying no, they do not want to go. This is it, and I realize the only way that the girls will go is if both are with me. So, we quickly move, assure the girls they will be fine, and before they know it, Christina is in my lap with Tracy sitting in front of her and we are headed for the dolphins. As the kayak glides effortlessly across the most incredibly beautiful, turquoise water, the girls giggle and watch the corals and bright tropical fish under our boat. As if by magic, we soar, as Ty silently paddles us farther into the ocean. In the distance, whales are breaching, leaving huge splashes of white water shooting into the air. The girls ooh and ah, as they agree to meet again for each other's birthdays and to email always.

Keep in mind, this is two four-year-old girls, who were cuddled in my lap, inches above the clear aqua ocean, sunlight reflecting in every direction. Suddenly, Christina gasps out loud, and then as delighted as I have ever heard anyone, she exclaims, "Oh, Oh my. The dolphins are right here."

And indeed, they had surfaced all around us, maybe twenty

of them, all at once. Several more swam under our boat. Ty dropped the paddle and we sat, watched and felt the dolphins. They swam off and then came out of the water directly in front of us about 25-feet out. As we watched, the dolphins formed a line of ten across, swimming straight at us, not diving under until they practically touched the boat. The girls were ecstatic and the show lasted for some time.

When the dolphins left us, Ty paddled back to shore. After unloading us girls, Ty took Steve and Nona out with the dolphins while the little girls and I joined Becky back at Baby Bay. Luka, who loves sitting in tide pool holes filled by buckets with water, stayed with us. When you see someone walking down the street after they have been touched by the dolphins, you know; you can see it.

Many times, I have asked, "Just been with the dolphins?"

As they bring you into focus with those clear, glassy eyes (the same as after an AquaCranial treatment coincidentally), you hear this rather breathless, "Yes," followed by a smile that beams so brightly, you would swear you could feel it. Christina and Tracy had the look. The girls continued to play and bond; Christina was happy and walking well. I did treatments on a couple of other people who joined us, and Steven and Nona had exquisite experiences with the dolphins. When they returned, Steven had an AquaCranial treatment. Nona had described her own treatment as being "like sleeping with her back pain gone when she woke up." Steven referred to feeling as if he had been hallucinating; evaluating his system, bones, and tissues. I wish, yet again, I had the funding to hire other therapists, so that parents could begin treatment right away, along with their children.

The Hawaiians have what they call "Hooponopono." Very loosely, the idea is to bring the whole family together to find out why the keiki (child) is sick or whatever the problem. I find this, of course, to be true. These parents have been through a very scary thing, waiting for their child to die, as she continues to experience desperate measures to save her. She told her parents early-on that she liked Rebecca as "she makes me feel good. And she doesn't stick me with needles and stuff."

While her parents believe I should do this full time, as I am good at it, my path includes nature and peace for the family, as well as treatments for the children. I have created a way to give something that is just not possible to obtain in a hospital setting. Our goal is to have our own boat, with staff, for a full time ocean clinic for children. Doctors, such as Christina's, who are open to helping the child and willing to "prescribe" Craniosacral so that insurance will cover the treatments, are becoming more and more available.

(Note: Cetacea Bleu, Inc., has never, ever, charged for treating children. We do often recommend follow-up care with a therapist in the child's area, which can be covered by insurance. An adjunct to other therapies, including drugs, CST is usually the least expensive.)

As the day winds down, we begin to pack up. With both arms full, I step into a lava hole, twist my foot, and begin to fall. Turning in what seems like slow motion, I fall in what seems to be the best way, catching my weight with my hand. Unfortunately, a lava "spike" drives a deep hole in my hand. I sit a moment, assure the kids that I am fine, and walk out to my truck, blood spurting. I would hate to throw up in front of the kids. Ty and I head home as all the kids go to the condo for more play. We agree to see the family for dinner that evening. While the others prepare dinner, Christina informs me that she does not want her final treatment. To persuade her, I ask her to help me, as it will be different doing a treatment with my hurt hand. She agrees, if we stay standing on the balcony. Two minutes into the treatment, Christina asks to lie down for the rest of the session. She continues to talk, suggesting ways to help my hand, as I evaluate her system. I would never give false hope. For the time being, however, she is, no doubt, a changed girl.

She began walking better the first day. When her parents asked her earlier in the day how her legs were doing, Christina told them, "Great! I am getting stronger every day."

Most of all the family is living every day together, instead of waiting to die. I do not know what will happen to Christina. As I said earlier, I have had cases where much more dramatic healing has occurred, but none could ever be as touching as Christina. She taught me to optimize, not necessarily strengthen. While I talked with Christina's parents, she played with Ty... doing summersaults. The sun was setting, and, yes, it was beautiful.

***It has been three years since Christina came to swim with the dolphins as her dying wish. Her parents recently emailed her picture and a drawing she had done of "The dolphins that healed me."

CHAPTER 5
DOLPHIN ETIQUETTE

"Nineteen centuries ago, Plutarch, a Greek moralist and biographer, made this statement: "To the dolphin alone, beyond all other, nature has granted what the best philosophers seek: friendship for no advantage."

We have been blessed with both human and cetacean friendship through our work. That is not always easy when you consider the emotional challenges healing a family can bring. What a joy, though, when, after all the hard work is done, a beautiful friendship emerges, along with the therapeutic advances for the child. Sometimes, it is not easy for parents to hear what I have to say, or to move through the personal growth that I have seen take place in some parents after they have brought their children for therapy. Most parents do not meet me until they arrive with their child for treatment. Sometimes, they have a language barrier to cross; English not being their first language. Many are living a life that was not what they expected. Most of us assume our children will be born perfect. Instead, they spend time with doctors and technicians. Then they meet this American woman who talks to dolphins and takes children into the ocean to be closer to whales. It is amazing how they even find me.

I introduce concepts to these parents that are completely foreign to most of them. My stories are pretty outrageous and hard to believe, until you are sitting next to me when a whale makes a 90% turn, picks her baby up on her nose, and carries the baby whale to my kayak. That happened with one Mama,

Stephanie, when she brought her daughter, Sylvy, from Germany for treatment.

It had been a challenge for Stephanie to work with me from the beginning. Some days, the bay is full of dolphins. Some days you would swear a dolphin never existed in the bay. Some days, the dolphins play hide and seek. Some times, they swim as far from you as possible, and some days, they surround you and interact for hours. There is never any way to tell how the interaction will happen. They could be here today and gone tomorrow. They could be there 30 days straight. They could be gone 30 days. I call it "dolphin waiting," instead of dolphin watching. After years of swimming in the same place, you accept the days of no dolphins as one day closer to a day with dolphins. Since I spend hundreds of days a year in the ocean, I have a lot of experiences and many thousand hours of dolphin swim time logged.

I prayed for dolphins the first time Stephanie's family came out with us. We did make contact. It was sporadic and fleeting. The wind and the waves were up and it was not easy to swim with the dolphins. Several times after that first experience, we took out the kayaks and found no dolphins.

"Sure you have dolphins look you in the face, swim close enough to touch you," she would say.

My husband, Ty, and Sylvy's daddy, Dimitri, learned to dive deeper and deeper. The turtles swam right up to us and played. Sylvy became bolder with her treatments and her deepwater swimming. There is something very cool, being a mile from shore in about a 100-feet of water with this little two-year-old chasing you around, laughing and shouting something that sounded like, "un da toaw, un da taow." She means, "Dive deeper, dive deeper."

She loves to be obeyed. I dove deeper. Sylvy spoke only German when we first met. In the weeks that we went waiting for dolphins, Sylvy learned many words.

"Paddle, paddle, paddle," she would rhythmically intone, as she moved the huge yellow paddle with her tiny hands.

Of course, in the beginning, I would move the paddle, my huge hands just outside of her baby hand.

"Hand," she would say, pushing the paddle and giving me a look that left no doubt that I would do what she wished. Sylvy would not let me touch her in the beginning, so I convinced her just to let me hold out her hand.

"Hand" I would say as I gently lifted her arm and treated her through her "hand.   Several treatments passed before she would willingly give me more. Sylvy was my challenge and my blessing. She taught me from the very beginning. She learned more English words, and we all paddled around in our kayaks. Six, seven weeks later, still no dolphins on the days Stephanie and Dimitri joined us. It did not help when Ty and I would go out with someone else, or alone, and swim with dolphins for hours the day before or after our trips with their family.

"Sure you swam with a 100 dolphins yesterday, and they recognized you, of course," Stephanie would say sarcastically.

She did not believe me, until the day of her AquaCranial class. I had a serious talk with the dolphins the day before. If I was going to keep telling people how the dolphins talk to me, teach me, work with me, the dolphins were going to have to be present physically as well as multidimensionally. Within minutes of the start of class, the dolphins arrived. We all swam deeper into the bay. The pod came to us and quickly split so that two or three dolphins were eye-to-eye with each class participant. The dolphins hung suspended in the water making deep eye contact. Debra was the first to pop. You could see the wave of emotion overcoming her before she melted in tears. The dolphins were going and getting disoriented swimmers and bringing them back to the pod of people and dolphins swimming together.

On one of these retrievals, the dolphins had brought Stephanie and Brian back to the group, the dolphins leaping and spinning in the air high above the water. Later, Stephanie had melted into my eyes as she said; "NOW I understand! The dolphins were WITH me."

KISSING WHALES HEALING DOLPHINS

Being with and swimming with dolphins is a far cry from chasing after dolphins in the water. The dolphins play many ways and swimming in the pod with them is unbelievably blissful. I would like to explain this in a way that people will perhaps get a little about dolphin etiquette. There is so much more to swimming with dolphins than snorkeling to look at fish. Dolphins will interact with you in an intelligent way. Have a bit of sensitivity to them and you will open a whole new world for yourself. Most tourists go for the "money shot," chasing the dolphins to "capture" a photo. "Taking" is illegal. To keep the ocean open for dolphin/human interaction, we need to develop a more conscious way to interact. This will save you a very expensive ticket from Ranger Rick at the end of your swim, as well as expand the quality of your dolphin experience. I am a certified marine mammal naturalist. I wanted to know more about the dolphins since they were obviously going to keep me busy. The dolphins at one particular Bay have worked with me for over a decade. I have documented there daily for three nonconsecutive years.

One year, when the dolphins did come into the bay, 90% of the time, it was between 7:00 and 9:00 a.m. That is not true for the year 2001. Twenty-five percent of the time it is after 11:00 a.m. when the dolphins arrive—IF they arrive. A few years ago, you could go MONTHS without seeing another human in the bay. The slopes of Haleakula Mountain swoop down towards LaPerouse Bay to touch the sea with lava rock that are hundreds of years old; pouring into the ocean as if it is still flowing. Six hundred people once lived in the lava rock village of Keniolio beside the sea. They would walk up the mountain to trade fish for vegetables. Their presence is so strong it took me a couple of years of visiting to be able to come all the way in to the village. I would live there now if they would let me.

Next to the Heiau, (a Hawaiian temple), is supposedly the strongest spot on the planet for releasing negative energy. I have seen people come to it from all over the world—Monks in orange robes, Hawaiians in full regalia, tourists told to pray on the spot, and others drawn there not knowing why. I have even seen sacred ceremonies filmed there, the day AFTER I dreamed it. Haleakula volcano is considered a very sacred spot on the planet. It is not dead. It has been a bit over 200 years since the last spurt of black lava flowed down the mountain, which is now surrounded by emerald Kiawe trees and plenty of deep, green, grasses from the Fall rains. It could flow again.

I had a dream that it did and some month's later, geologists were checking a "hot spot" on the mountain, which had been in my dreams. It did not erupt and they went away several months ago. Last night there was an earthquake that seemed to flow from the mountain, waves across the island to the sea. It shook the whole house, swaying to the side. After living in California, I cannot mistake an earthquake. If the mountain does send lava flowing again, it will be interesting to see what happens. Perhaps, I will live on the lava fields of Maui before it is all over.

If you come here to swim with dolphins, keep an eye on the waves and keep an eye on the mountain. Many, many people now come here to swim with the dolphins. Too many people, no doubt. The kayaks filled with tourists slathered in reef-killing sunscreen. I have been run over by kayaks, kicked in the head and body-slammed as tourists fight to get "closer" to the dolphins. Then they pop out of the water wondering where the dolphins went. DUH! You chased them away. Swim with them. Do not chase them. If you charge at them and they suddenly change direction, not only did you blow your chance to hang out with them, you just broke the law.

On the other hand, if they are swimming with you, feeding, mating, and even sleeping, no law is broken, as no behaviors are altered in the pod. It can be mind boggling to be swept into the hypnotic movements of a sleeping pod—over you, under you, next to you. If you pay attention, you can tell which ones are sleeping. I can "feel" the steady, rhythmic flow of their energy throughout the water. One or two dolphins on the outer edge stay awake to guide and protect the pod. I have even had them swim next to me, using my field to guide their movements. One dolphin will slide up next to me, their body touching mine, the next dolphin touching that dolphin until the entire pod of dolphins is linked together. They close their eyes and follow me by feel. They feel me and trust me that much. Do not get me wrong. I am no doubt, at least partly responsible for the dolphin swimmers. I have seen the healing that happens, and even managed to document some interesting facts. I truly wish to protect the resource (the dolphins and the ocean), protect the swimmers, and encourage multiple species communications. The dolphins are used to multi-specie communication with eels, octopus, fish, and other mammals, whales, and monk seals. It is humans who are less experienced in multi-species communication, with the exception of their communication with their pets and other domesticated animals.

It is not the humans' fault if they do not know what they are doing. Education is the big key. Easily, 100 kayaks now launch on a busy day. About four years ago, the kayak business exploded. Guides came here from Florida or other places already overrun with too many kayak companies. A fresh market—we were. Many of the guides are fairly good about giving their clients enough clarity so that everyone has a good experience. The more you tune in to the dolphins, the more fun you can have with them. If you dive down and twirl around, there is a good chance that one or more will begin twirling as well. I have seen five spotted dolphins in the Bahamas surround Ty on all sides, each one less than a foot from his body. Every dolphin slowly swirls around and around; Ty turning exactly the same, the entire group, man and dolphins, a revolving carousel, slowly drifting down to the bottom of the ocean and then back towards the surface. Sun beams cutting through aqua water so clear it seems as if they are floating in space.

If a dolphin wants to touch you, it will. If it wants you to touch it, a dolphin will slide up next to you, touching skin to skin. I love it. Some days you see the occasional naked body swimming with the dolphins. NEVER, ever, reach out to touch the dolphins. This is considered harassment, and can be considered aggressive by the dolphins, as they have no arms and it will most likely cause them to scatter quickly. If the dolphins want to move away, at 60 miles an hour, they will out swim you. This does not mean it is not rude to wake them up and make them out swim you. The saddest thing I have seen with the dolphins is the fear in their eyes as they came towards me after escaping a pod of humans enthusiastically/aggressively chasing the poor dolphins into the rocks. It was really horrible. I saw what was happening, and even though it was a pod that I knew and was having a great time swimming with prior to the crowd arriving, I moved off to the side by a couple of hundred yards. It was disgusting to watch the humans cut off the path, herding the dolphins closer and closer to shore. It was as bad as any National Geographic special on hunting.

As the warriors moved closer to their prey, spreading the human net alongside the dolphins, and then pushing them into the rocks, I could not believe my eyes. Suddenly, the frantic dolphins burst through a hole in the wall of people and shot into the open. As they came to me, I saw looks in their eyes that I hope to never see again. People wonder why I sometimes put myself between them and the dolphins, and plead with them to back off of bit. I spend hours observing both cetacean and human behaviors. Remember, Ranger Rick is watching you too. The dolphins love to come up and check YOU out. They will look right at you. I just hang out and look right back. Since few people will look another person in the eye and just relax into that looking, it is no wonder they do not even think about doing it with a dolphin. Try it.

I just relax, hang out, and see what mood the dolphins are in. They set the stage for the interaction. Some days, I am just swimming along and here come the dolphins. We swim along together, one or more may swim up to say "Hi" nose to nose, diving deeper and deeper down towards the bottom. I love to turn on my side and flash my tummy at the dolphins. The ones who come to the bay most often turn on their sides and flash their tummies at me. It is our sign. Now, before you think I am hallucinating, not all dolphins will mimic this behavior with me. Only the pods I am with regularly. But, dolphins are smart and they are playful. If you kick back and let them take the lead, you can have some fun. They love toys and will sometimes bring a leaf so that you can play "catch the leaf" with them. Sometimes, they like to fly past so you have a brief encounter. I have seen them lead groups of people all over the bay and back, and a good time was had by all. Unfortunately, I have seen very aggressive, obviously fit people do their best to be leader of the pack. If the dolphins are actually swimming with slower swimmers, the Olympians will run the dolphins off. It is really not about who can swim fastest, it is more about who the DOLPHINS WANT to swim with them.

I have been swimming along in a pod of dolphins, cruising the bay with them, when we have been joined by a group of tourists who suddenly "discover" that the dolphins are there. The people push and shove to get to them the fastest. I always allow some space, three or four feet, between me and the dolphins, when we are cruising. They move closer if they want to be personal and touch. On the freeway, I like to leave some extra room between me and the car ahead. Ever do that, and suddenly, in zooms someone, bumper to bumper now, to snag the empty space? Same thing happens with the dolphins. Leave the slightest bit of space and someone wants to be CLOSER to the dolphins. Problem is dolphins like to turn, sway, and swirl, so if you get too close, they will have to alter their pattern. It's not just the dolphins you are crowding next to, but the entire pod of 20 to 100. It is not comfortable.

Part of the glory of swimming in the ocean is that it is big enough to make some wide turns. If you feel the dolphins, give them some space and watch them, you can comfortably and easily begin to move with them. Being accepted into the pod is an immense gift. The peace and fluidity, the unity, are unmatched. Once you are in, you are in. You belong. They will feed the baby, make love with each other and all the while, look you in the eye. I love it when they swim all around me, popping their heads out of the water to look me in the eye in the bright sunshine. Then we all dive back under. It is such a cool game, "see me look at you under the water, see me look at you out of the water." We are all just swimming along, not a care in the world.

I actually listen to what they tell me in addition to all of the above. Sometimes they say, swim here quick, other times, kayak to the other side of the bay. Then we swim around together, slowly, then sprinting, then slow for a cool down. The dolphins will stay an hour or two; sometimes longer. Those days, they are my "personal trainers." I almost feel that I should tip them with a fish but, RULE #37... Never feed the dolphins.

CHAPTER 6
AQUACRANIAL

"A quaCranial Therapy's gentle touch facilitates flight into another realm. You are immersed in what seems like another dimension, weightless, fluid, cool; experiencing a hypnotic sense of timelessness. A facilitated unfolding into calm, deep, relaxation where the body, mind, and spirit can rest at peace."

I originated AquaCranial Therapy, an extension of the Sutherland-Sills method of Craniosacral Therapy, with the guidance and interaction of the cetaceans. An advanced modality, it is a mix of osteopathic-based Craniosacral manipulations, dolphin therapy movements, visionary emotional release work, meridian balancing, yogic stretches, and extreme hydrotherapy, developed through years of cetacean research. AquaCranial decompresses the spine, cranium, bones, and tissue. Balancing the Craniosacral system eliminates physical stress from the body, acquired since birth up until the present time. If you bend a garden hose in half while it is turned on, no water will flow until you release the bend in the hose. Same principal holds true. If you hold your phone with your neck and shoulder, lift your hip to carry baby, lift your shoulder to hold your purse, sleep on the plane in a weird position, fall off your bike or skis, etc., you create small bends or restrictions in the hose-like membrane surrounding the Craniosacral fluid and it cannot flow. Just like the water and the bent garden hose.

Close your eyes a moment. Listen and feel your breathing. Notice the rhythm. After a moment, shift your attention to your heartbeat and rhythm. It is a completely different movement. Next, look for the other rhythm, the third movement that is not your heart or lungs. Your body will appear to empty and fill. This third rhythm is the Craniosacral rhythm. When you die, after your heart stops beating, after your lungs quit breathing, approximately 20 minutes later, your cranial sacral rhythm will cease. This is why it is called the primary respiratory mechanism in the body. The acknowledgement of a vital life force is at the heart of the Craniosacral concept and was referred to as the Breath of Life by Dr. William Sutherland, who considered it to be the principle that maintains balance and order in the body.

Dr. Sutherland, an osteopath, is the founder of Craniosacral study. Discovering that the skull had what appeared to be "gills like a fish," he began experimenting by creating restrictions in various parts of his own skull. His wife would document any personality changes, headaches, etc. Once he discovered that the cranial sutures are meant for respiration and are not fused, he spent 50 years exploring the significance of the Craniosacral motion. He developed and taught cranial osteopathy until his death in 1954. I was introduced to cranial osteopathy in the 70's by Randolph Stone, himself a student of Dr. Sutherland. There are many schools that teach various aspects of Craniosacral Therapy. Dr. John Upledger, in the seventies, developed a program offering Craniosacral training to a variety of licensed professionals who were not necessarily osteopathic physicians, after he had seen substantial results in autistic children receiving treatments with him. His Institute has done extensive research proving the value of Cranial Sacral Therapy in a variety of situations.

Hugh Milne, author of two excellent books, The Heart of Listening Book 1 and Book 2, said the cranial sacral system is both the densest form of spirit and the lightest form of matter. I like to think that means this is where you can literally, physically touch spirit. He also said you can never go too deep, only too fast; a good thing to remember. Sutherland refers to the Craniosacral fluid as "where the photons of light literally step down into" the body. In AquaCranial Therapy, we use Cranio-sacral manipulations developed by Dr. Sutherland and by me, facial releases, and dolphin movements, to assess and treat the Craniosacral system, which consists of the membranes and cerebrospinal fluid that surrounds and protects the brain. This system extends down from the bones of the face, skull and mouth, which make up the cranium, to the tailbone area (sa-crum). The Craniosacral system influences the development and performance of the brain and spinal cord.

We then continue to assess and treat all joints in the body, including the extremities, to encourage further releases from tissue, fluid, and bone. Since ocean water is close to the makeup of embryonic fluid, the comfort and safety of the womb is replicated. Wave motion helps the spine release with gentle movements synchronized to the wave. Movement is fluid and effortless. The water creates a gentle compression on the muscles of the client. The body is subject to 15% of the gravity in water that it would have to withstand on land. Three-dimensional movements are much easier than on the table, and some movements in AquaCranial simply could not be done on a therapy table.

There is an aspect of sensory insulation in the ocean similar to the isolation tanks created by John Lilly, which contained salt water. The insulation of electrical waves is particularly impor-tant as we work to shift the electromagnetic field of the body. Heated and mineral waters are used to further enhance the re-lease of bones and tissues with a specific intermixing of hot and cold-water treatments. Restrictions or imbalances in the Cranio-sacral system caused by birth, childhood injuries, sports, stress, illness, repetitive movements or medications, to name a few, could potentially cause any number of neurological disabilities. The AquaCranial therapist encourages your Craniosacral system to release the effect of stresses from your nervous system through manipulations as gentle as one gram or even less.

This therapy is incredibly deep and powerful while still be-ing very gentle and noninvasive; alternating stillness and movements dance you through the waters, sometimes softly, sometimes with a more compelling touch. When you strengthen the body's ability to heal itself by freeing the Craniosacral system of restrictions, you also alleviate a wide range of illness, pain, and dysfunction. Things such as chronic neck and back pain, headaches, chronic fatigue syndrome, scoliosis, emotional difficulties, learning disabilities, TMJ syndrome, chronic fatigue, post-traumatic stress disorder, sleep apnea, traumatic brain and spinal cord injuries, motor coordination impairments, central nervous system disorders, and more have responded to Craniosacral Therapy. There are institutes that compile reams of research about the benefits of treating the Craniosacral system. I mention the challenges that I personally have treated with success. The benefits of treating the cranial sacral system include: resistance to disease, better health in general, and a looser, more relaxed, body. We have only done soft research with AquaCranial Therapy, but the increased flow of the Craniosacral fluid and the release of restrictions during the treatments are tangible. Since the fluid flowing through the dural tube would be restricted simply by lying on a treatment table, the benefit of lying in water with no outside dural tube restriction is obvious. Our experience to date, which consists of tens of thousands of treatments, suggests one water treatment is as effective as three conventional table treatments.

Since AquaCranial Therapy is experienced differently by everyone, I am including some comments here from clients and journalists:

"She took me straight to Heaven. It was the most spiritual and memorable part of my trip to Hawaii. Rebecca brought the whales to sing for me."
—Ari Foxwell, Germany, age 80

"I experienced the treatment at the Four Seasons Maui with Rebecca. It was the most significant treatment on the menu."

KISSING WHALES HEALING DOLPHINS

—Kim Knapp, Day Spa owner, Florida

"In the womblike ocean, with Goff spinning me and rocking me gently, I fall into a deep state of relaxation like nothing I have ever experienced."
—Editor in Chief, Coast Magazine

"Rebecca held my hand and swam me face to face with the dolphins. She put a pillow under my head to treat me while the dolphins swam all around us. It was the most amazing experience of my life. I could not stop smiling all day."
—Katy, Spa Receptionist, Manele Bay Resort, Lanai Hawaii

"I am on day 14 of no headaches (after 20 years of daily headaches). I feel so great. Thank you for changing my life."
— Jennifer Payne, Texas

"Thank you so much for the beautiful gifts… opening my mind, body, and soul. I feel totally blessed to have come to Maui and met you."
—Emily Kaph, Yoga Teacher
Owner of Bikram Yoga Studios, New York

"Wearing a wetsuit in thigh-high water, clients float weightlessly into alpha bliss with an air pillow tucked under their neck and gentle support from a therapist. Profoundly relaxing, AquaCranial decompresses both spine and cranium and releases tension and energy blockage in the entire body."
—Ann Wycoff, Spa Magazine

"Thank you for the pleasure and privilege of being the subject of a class exercise and clinic. The experiences were brand new to me and no doubt advancing healing arts."
—Elizabeth Frazee, Indiana

"Rebecca cradled the back of my head in her hands as she guided my body through alternating patterns of stillness and

movement. During the stillness, her touches under my head, on my forehead, and around my jaw, were almost imperceptible. Integrated with gentle pulls through the water and wavelike rocking from head to toe and side to side, Rebecca facilitated a freedom in movement and a level of relaxation and stress release I had never experienced. It was a feeling of movement and sensation without any physical effort, like dancing while standing still. ...The therapy itself felt so gentle and non-intrusive, I was quite shocked by the deep level of relaxation I felt afterwards."
—Courtney Mather, Healing Retreats and Spas Magazine

"What can we say? You left us "speechless." Your energy is plentiful. Thank you."
—Diane Trieste, Corporate Spa Treatment Director, Canyon Ranch Health Resorts

"Today's vacation spas are no longer fat farms for the rich and famous. Instead, they're catering to a growing desire for full scale pampering ...while tykes are learning the hula on the beach, parents can head into the surf for an AquaCranial massage. ...the therapist cradles your legs, using gentle massage at key pressure points to relieve tension. ...great freedom in being supported in the ocean on very deep level..."
—International Newsweek Magazine

We usually make three passes over the body during treatment. The first pass is to release the daily stresses and tensions, with each pass going progressively deeper. Although we tell the client they will be somewhat altered at the end of the treatment, we catch them all by surprise. At the Four Seasons Maui, we wrote on the promo that you would be somewhat altered at the end of the treatment, and bookings from L.A. went up something like 500%. Rocker, Michael Anthony, bass player for the Van Halen Band, was shocked as he had to be helped from the water. After lying quietly for a few minutes, he suddenly jumped up and said, "I feel GREAT! I am ready to party."

When doing a hot stone treatment on a very well known English Rocker, he asked me what I was doing to his head. When I replied, "Craniosacral Therapy," he sat up suddenly, looked at me, and excitedly asked if I had ever done "that AquaCranial Therapy."

"It REALLY stoned me out," he said, and then he lay back with a look of wonder in his eyes. We see that a lot, the "look of wonder" after a treatment.

It is very important that the client be prepared ahead of time, especially if their use of the English language is limited. I did a treatment on a journalist from OZ Magazine. I tried to explain before the treatment, but "altered" is not a Japanese term. I said, "A little like being a bit tipsy after drinking."

She quickly denied," Oh no, I never drink."

I took her into the ocean and proceeded with the treatment. Some people are simply very relaxed during the treatment. Others have compared it to an acid trip with colored lights and visions. Chris, my favorite backup when I was at the Seasons, worked at the beach, and watched the treatments and the walkouts.

"It is very different for everyone, isn't it? Some people come out just really relaxed. But with others, you can tell it touched their souls."

When the journalist from OZ sat up and realized just how altered she was, from the look in her eyes, I would say that she was actually a bit frightened.

"This is normal," I said to reassure her.

She turned to face me with a wild look in her eyes. "This is NOT normal," she insisted.

I helped her to a chair, wrapped her in a warm blanket, and told her to close her eyes. "You will be fine in a moment, just relax with your eyes closed."

I stayed close enough to "feel" the client who was now nestled warmly on a chaise lounge, which we had prepared in advance. We have the lounge chair covered with thick terry cloth, and a towel is provided to wrap the guest's head and shoulders.

They have been removed from their wetsuit and helped into a plush terry robe, covered with another body length towel, and finally, a fluffy warm blanket on top of everything for the cuddle factor. It is like being in the most decadent comfy bed on one of the most beautiful beaches in the world. Early morning streaks of sun reflect off the mirror-like surface of the deep cobalt ocean. The stretch of fine, golden sand is usually fairly empty in the morning, except for the lithe bodies following Kamala through a flow of yoga asana's in the alcove where the lava rocks rise out of the ocean to form a natural wall.

Five minutes later, I asked her, "All better now?"

She smiled beautifully and peacefully at me, "Yes, it was very good, thank you."

"I tried to warn you!" I told her.

We both laughed softly.

The "Trippin with May ling Show" from the Oxygen network did a segment on Hawaii. As I walked May Ling to the water, I explained that she would be a bit altered at the end. She just rolled her eyes and gave me a sarcastic look like, "Oh Really!"

Later, as I helped her walk from the ocean, she looked at me in wonder and said, "That really was altering. Very tranquil."

"Don't worry," I told her. "It will pass in a few minutes."

"Oh no, I like it!" she exclaimed.

So, we put her off to the side at the secluded end of the beach, next to the lava wall, wrapped in a blanket on her lounge chair under the cabana Chris set up for her. Although it only takes about five to fifteen minutes for the electrical system to finish its reorganization into a more coherent pattern, some guests choose to spend more time relaxing in their cozy nest, enjoying the sounds of the ocean waves washing on the shore, and the feeling of soft clarity and relaxation caused by the negative ions in the warm ocean air.

I have had children swim around their parents during treatment, dogs swim around their owners, and one tiny dog actually swam out into the ocean to us and climbed right on his owner's tummy. This little puppy was so precious, soaked to the skin, still dripping wet, and watching my every move. Shaking from the exertion of the swim, precariously balanced, the puppy stayed perched on his human float until the end of the treatment. The funniest to me was when I worked on a very well known, currently hot, rock star. I am used to the idiosyncrasies of my star clients and accommodate their hectic schedules and special needs however I can. Since many travel with an entourage, I have extra seats, etc., prepared. The personal trainer/bodyguard of this particular star took his work to heart. He came into the water with us and swam circles around us to protect his "man" from tourists or whatever else might approach. After the treatment, the rocker, who could barely walk going into the ocean due to a recent car accident, came out asking if he could lift weights now. He told his trainer it was really great, but it was the weirdest treatment.

A client who was later referred to me by them told me, "My insurance company said I was so screwed up that they would pay for me to see a witch doctor, if it would help. (Superstar rocker) told me to come see you!"

Two amazing therapists, Debra and David, began free clinics for children on Kauai after their basic training. Debra sings beautiful Hawaiian chants to the children as she starts her treatment and her keiki (children) will ask for it, if another therapist does not start with the chant. David was a dentist for many years and I will never forget the look on his face the first day of training. Everyone arrived for class, parking in an area next to the ocean, after driving 25-minutes through lava fields. Carrying their lunches, water bottles, and other personal belongs over a rock wall and across lava rocks; they came to sand chairs set up on the flat, black rock next to the ocean in the middle of nowhere. This was my first meeting with most of the students.

Most of our interactions are emails prior to this first in-person event. As students arrive, some carpooling together, others arriving at about five minute intervals, there is light conversation as people settle their personal belongings around their chair—no tables at this class. Hugs and hellos to mostly new friends; some have met us before. We videotape all trainings, as they are experimental and experiential in nature. Students sometimes leave with a manual and are always given specific training and protocols, but the training method is as fluid as the dolphins in the water.

Most people have flown in the day before and are still adjusting to arrival. It is an hour drive winding around the steep pali high above the foaming ocean from the Napali Coast, or from the cool and rainy mountain upcountry, half an hour from the sunny beaches of the Wailea resorts, to where we train. Most have been awake since five or five thirty this morning. There are sleepy faces sipping tea, juices, and coffee; most still just thinking about waking up. It is so beautiful at 7:00 a.m., pink light streaking the violet and pale blue skies. The sun has not peaked over the edge of the mountain yet, so the sunlight is still diffused. Here come the dolphins.

"Okay, everyone. Put on your fins. The dolphins are here and we are going in."

To the left of the tiny secluded bay where we train is a larger bay; now the site of jumping dolphins.

"Just head straight out there," I tell the confused but excited faces, pointing about 300 yards out into the ocean.

Meanwhile, my husband Ty has set up the two-man kayak that I will use as a lifeguard station for easy visual of all the participants and everything else in the bay, boats, waves, and dolphins. Everyone follows us in their kayaks. The dolphins disappear. I call people over.

"Okay, partner up and do a still point on each other."

Everyone looks at me. Again, David's look was the funniest. I am sure this was nothing like dental school. We are in about 20-feet of water. I laugh at the looks.

"It's easy. One person lies down and floats in the water. The other person then does a still point anywhere on your partner's body."

Gamely, they pair off, one person per pair, floating in the clear turquoise water above the coral reef. We lose the first of many masks and snorkels. Fortunately, Ty can now dive 50-feet and will retrieve them later. As everyone relaxes and explores, the energy becomes altered in a tangible way. Soon, everyone is surrounded by the dolphins they did not notice come in until they were two feet away.

"Now, you are getting it," I say softly from my perch on a green kayak, floating in the middle of them all. "Swim with your new friends. Remember to check the shore to see where you are periodically."

Everyone gets somewhat altered while swimming with dolphins. You can go far out into the deep rather quickly without even realizing it. After the Dolphin 101, we returned to our Oceanside classroom to meet each other and discuss what we had learned so far. I then gave a demo in shallow water, implementing all the little details that make the big differences in water works. We discussed the energetic difference of working in 15 to 20-feet of water, the gentlest of spaces, and 5-feet of water, where the therapist was more grounded and capable of more control of movement. In really deep water, the psyche is affected more deeply. There the work is more about consciousness. The therapist may wear no fins and in 200-feet or more of water, flows with the whim of the ocean.

The Basic Training course for AquaCranial Therapy is just that—basic. Participants will add their personal touch, integrating what they have learned in other trainings into the basic protocol we teach. I will show them at what stage they may want to implement the mouth work they know. Or how to use myofascial release techniques to more effectively release the membranes. Some techniques, such as the whale rock©, allow for a greater freedom of movement within the Craniosacral system of the body. As with rocking whales, it stretches muscles, increases circulation, loosens the spine and adjusts equilibrium. (Whales are rocked when they are beached and helped back into the water, in case you were wondering why on earth anyone would rock a whale.)

The whale rock© opens both the lower lumbar area of the spine and the mid-thoracic area in a way which allows great releases of Craniosacral fluid flow and more freedom of movement in the spine above and below the point of contact for the manipulation. Humans used to spend more time in water bodies large enough to move around in when we bathed in streams and waterfalls. Bathtubs and shower stalls restrict our water movement and we lose natural fluidity; this shifts our equilibrium. Our bodies are more locked in the box. The whale rock allows many systems of the body to "remember" to be more fluid and to "loosen up." It definitely shifts the equilibrium in the body to receive an AquaCranial treatment.

After they finish training, students do 10 to 15 practice sessions to get to know what it is they are doing. I love Debra. She is so Kauai. Here is an email from her, telling the story of her "practice" session.

> "Dear Rebecca,
>
> Fifteen sessions later, I feel so blessed. I am learning that it is OK for work to feel easy and fun! Last night, I shared my first "full moon" AquaCranial. This was the third session for my friend who is a gifted shaman. (This week she has become my "ground crew" and supports integration with a seashell lay-out. When I experienced it personally, it felt powerfully deepening.) During her AquaCranial session last night, she achieved whale rocking fluidity like I have never felt before. Later, she shared the nature of her emotional tumult, which ensued mid-session. She was told it is time for her to work with an entirely new group of power animals and let the others go. Whale came to her!
> With much aloha,
> Debra

CHAPTER 7
500 DOLPHINS

Today was stunningly amazing. I had heard of people being surrounded by 500 dolphins. It was one dolphin experience I had not had myself—until today. My student Lori's buddy, Binger, called early. He said Lori had been up until 3:00 a.m. with excruciating knee pain and would not be going kayaking, but he would meet Ty and I at the bay. We arrived right behind him. As soon as we parked, Ty walked over to take Binger a sweet, juicy mango for a pre-kayak breakfast. It took about five seconds to see that the dolphins were here—right close to shore, jumping and calling me out. I could feel my body full of joy and "tickles," which always meant I would have contact with the dolphins. I was filled with excitement hard to describe, and ran to the guys.

"Dolphins are here," Ty said.

"I know. Let's GO!" I wailed.

We quickly set up our kayak. Binger was adjusting his gear as he walked into the water. We had brought two 2-man kayaks, so he would be swimming without Lori to fill the second seat. The dolphins had been swimming all around the kayaks and human swimmers, up close and personal. They headed directly to our kayak. Suddenly, they turned sharply and headed quickly out of the bay. We were in our kayaks and followed. About 20 feet away, we saw that Michael, one of the regular dolphin swimmers who came to this bay, was swimming with them. Some days, he appeared to push them, but today, they were surrounding him and very definitely swimming right with him. It is an awesome thing. Ty and I have been spoiled many, many times; being the only one with the dolphins. Today, Michael was in bliss—just him and the dolphins. We did not want to spoil the moment, so hung back and watched him and the dolphins loving the day. After a bit, two other pods of dolphins appeared, and the ones with Michael cut over to join them. Michael looked up at us and smiled. We paddled closer.

"Awesome," we all said at once.

We chatted a moment and then left Michael to follow the dolphins around the edge of the lava flow. They seemed to beckon us to follow.

"What are you doing?" Ty asked.

We did not usually go out this way with them. Today, the water was flat and glassy and I could not resist the call of the dolphins. I was fascinated, watching them cruise in semicircles to the lava wall and back into the ocean.

"I want to follow them," I said.

After a bit, they turned again and headed back into the bay. About twenty kayaks with two tourists each were rounding the corner. Maybe 100 dolphins now surrounded us.

"I'm in," Ty said, sliding soundlessly into the water.

He was off and surrounded by dolphins in moments. There was no one except him, with dolphins in front, behind, all around. I watched the kayaks speed up and people prepare to jump in the water. It was a race, and they had just caught up to the prize, if they could just swim fast enough. It was all over their faces.

"Relax, this group is a bit shy, but hanging out. They are everywhere. Just, relax."

"We tell them and tell them," sighed the guide. "Then the moment they hit the water, they forget everything."

We have all seen it for years. It takes time to establish a relationship with the dolphins and learn to interact with them. It has been about 15 years for Ty and I with almost daily time in the ocean for quite a few years now. God has blessed us, no doubt. And today, the dolphins were spoiling us. The dolphins headed back around the corner into the bay again. There, they split into three pods heading in three directions. I thought Ty had gone with them, so I continued around the corner. Several dolphins came right up to my kayak and began playing with the boat and with me. These guys were playing under the front of my kayak, like they usually play on a boat, riding the wake. Looking up into my eyes, they invited me in. I went.

I slid into the water, holding onto the leash of my kayak, pulling it behind me. The dolphins surrounded me and we played for a bit. They made a turn and I saw several more dolphins swim up. When they all shot off in one direction, I looked up out of the water. They were swimming directly at Ty! As soon as I saw him, they disappeared.

"I cannot believe you just bailed on me!" He spat out as he swam up.

"I thought you were way ahead swimming with the dolphins. Like you usually are," I answered.

"What dolphins? I never saw any," he said, obviously agitated.

"Are you kidding me? They were all around you."

"That's what several other people I swam by said, but I could not see them." "Well, okay, they were not six inches from you. But when you have 100 dolphins surrounding you on all sides, even if they are 10 feet away, it is a pretty impressive sight."

"Well, maybe to you, but I could not see one dang dolphin and you left me. I think the dolphins are going to Ahihi."

"They seem to be collecting pods, and I get the same feeling. They are calling us to Ahihi. Let's Go."

"I told you we should get the boat earlier and take it out."

He was still peeved with me.

"I know, I know. I just wanted to be with them here too. It is like they are beginning to pod really big. Look, there must be 150 now."

We paddled the 10 minutes around the corner back to the car. Binger was still hanging out.

"I swam out, but they split immediately," he said.

We loaded up the kayaks and headed down the road to Ahihi. After passing a dive buddy, Ty headed back to show video of the Bahamas trip we had just finished. I looked for dolphins. Susan, another regular dolphin swimmer in this bay, just back from the mainland, was there looking for her "fix."

"I have to get into the water. Do you think they will come this way?" She asked.   "They had that feel," I said.

We chatted and giggled about her recent trip.

"There they are!" I shouted, as the dolphins rounded the corner.

They started leaping and spinning as if they were as excited as we were. I ran down the street. Ty was walking towards me.

"The dolphins are here."

"I know, I know. I was coming to get you."

We quickly unstrapped the kayak, hooked up the seats, paddles, and life jackets. The dolphins were flying.

"They are really on the move," Ty said.

"Go get your boat and meet us south of the Kealani Resort", the dolphins showed me, suddenly in my head.

"Maybe we should go get the boat and drop in up the coast a bit," I said to Ty.

"I have said that about a dozen times now," he said, giving me that sweet disgusted look he can get.

"There are hundreds of us gathering. We will surround the boat and you can travel with us a bit. Go get your boat."

Again, the dolphin pictures played in my head.

"Let's do it," I said as the giggles inside my body increased.

We drove half an hour back, with a stop for sandwiches. Binger went to get Lori as we hooked up the boat and headed out for gas. Twenty minutes later, we met at the boat launch and dropped in the boat. Would we find those dolphins we had left nearly an hour ago? Still the pictures of them surrounding us in my mind did not go away. Ten minutes later, we saw the dolphins. A big Pacific Whale Foundation Boat and a smaller boat painted with rainbows, galaxies, crystals and dolphins, were behind the dolphins. The captain of the smaller boat called out to us.

"They are on the move," said Captain Simone.

"We know. We left them in our kayaks at Big Beach when they sent us for our boat. They said they would be here with lots of friends. About 500 friends, actually," we shouted back to Simone.

On the way to the boat dock Ty had looked me directly in the eye and asked, "What would you do if 500 dolphins actually did show up like they showed you, exactly where there showed you?"

"I would…" Okay, not the best answer, but even after decades of visions proven to be correct, some are still pretty unreal. What if dolphins suddenly projected a picture into your head, of you surrounded in your boat by 500 dolphins in front of a specific resort? Would you pop over there, expecting the dolphins to be waiting? On the other hand, I have traveled halfway around the world to watch what the dolphins have told me they would do once I arrived wherever they sent me, and did what they proposed that I do. This time was no exception to the rule that the dolphins deliver.

For about a quarter-mile square, the ocean appeared full of dolphins. Small groups of 10 to 15 would cruise next to our feet, dangled over the side of the boat, swishing from side to side. After a few minutes, the dolphins would casually move off as another group took their place. Some playful pods would jump up to Simone, standing on the front of her boat before shooting across the waves to jump for us. We all moved along at idle speed. At one point, I could not stand it anymore.

"I am going in," I declared, jumping up and grabbing my fins and snorkel.

"They won't stop. You can tell they are on the move," Ty said startled. "You could never keep up."

I knew he was right. It had been two hours and the dolphins, all 500 or so, had stayed with us, moving us along at what we refer to as "traveling speed." They have many different behaviors. We have experienced this behavior both in Hawaii with the Spinner dolphins and in the Bahamas with the Spotted and Bottlenose dolphins. Sometimes, the dolphins are sleeping and during these times, they swim slowly. Sometimes, they want to play and interact with humans. It is very obvious. Other times, they are on the move; they are cruising. When in this mode, the dolphins will often play with the boat, but will not slow down to swim at "human speed." I had my fins and mask on.

"I know they won't stop, but I have to do it anyway. Come back for me." Those were my last words as I stuck the snorkel in my mouth and jumped overboard. Please remember I have spent my life in and on the water, and my husband is used to what I do. I went off in a way that I knew was well clear of the boat, safe for me, and safe for the boat. I was also well clear of the dolphins. Once I hit the ocean and plunged down through the waves, the dolphins closed in around me. I swear, they can smile. I just floated there while they swam around me, turning lazily to show off their style. By the time Ty turned the boat around and came back for me, several hundred dolphins had cruised over, under, and around me.

"Get in the boat, you nut," Ty said, laughing and shaking his head as he expertly circled the boat to pick me up. "I told you they would not stop."

"It was worth it," I beamed at him, tossing my fins into the boat and climbing the ladder.

"You are insane," Binger laughed at me once I was in.

"I won't do it again," I promised.

It only took me 20 years of hanging out with dolphins to end up in a group this big, so nobody has to worry about me doing it again anytime soon anyway. Sharks do hang with large pods sometimes, and a regular deep ocean swimmer was bit by a shark while he was swimming off Oahu with some dolphins last year. It does happen—this is Nature, not Disneyland.

The dolphins stayed with us about four hours, leaving us

just where we would turn off to the dock. They all turned in the opposite direction like one huge being, heading towards the sunset—or maybe open ocean. Who knows? Maybe they went to Lanai. Wherever they went, they did not return to the bay for over three weeks.

CHAPTER 8
TONES

Ty and I both awakened early today. I did not feel the dolphins would be in. At 6:15 a.m., we got in the truck anyway, already loaded with kayak and equipment, and headed to dolphin land. Everything is so green in Wailea, lots of golf courses and resorts sprinkled with mansions. In just minutes, we are in Makena. Deserts, cactus and kiawe' trees around the mansions. Two more minutes driving and then it is nothing but lava, desert, and ocean. Pretty gray and rough, the ocean shows no sign of dolphins when we pull up to the shore a few miles further. In five minutes, I am ready to leave "right now."

"Let's head to Ahihi," I say, kind of anxious for some reason, like I have a schedule to keep.

While we are driving, Ty starts telling me a story about the dolphins.

"They Shepard the fish who grow up in the bay. Then at a certain age, the dolphins round up all the akule and herd them into the little bay where you do clinics. The fishermen come and drop nets. Dolphins eat what they want, jumping easily over the nets, coming in and out. The fishermen believe the dolphins help them."

I vaguely remember Robert telling Ty this story when a bunch of us kayaked out with the dolphins a few days earlier.

"So, I started paying attention to what the dolphins were doing with the fish after hearing the story. There definitely is one that Sheppard's those fish. The dolphin had a large range he would work. He also used a tone I had not heard before.

When he would make the tone, a large bubble would elongate along his back until it reached his fin."

"You actually noticed a specific tone?" I asked him.

"Definitely. I had never heard them use it before and it was quite distinctive."

We had arrived at Ahihi. Before Ty could even park, I felt the urge to move on.

"Keep going, no dolphins here," I told him. "Funny, just this week I heard a tone that was different than any I had heard before."

We do not even realize that we have been recognizing the tones until we realize that we do NOT recognize a specific one. Once I actually notice a certain behavior however, the dolphins are much more active in whatever behavior it is, as if to help me with my studies. Now, they would sound a certain tone. I would guess who the tone was "naming," and then I would look to see if that person had come to me in the water. After awhile I could easily identify who the dolphins were signaling me was coming in my direction by the tone or name the dolphins had associated with specific people.

For instance, one day I had the "feeling" that they wanted me to stay to see something, but there was also one clear tone I had not heard before that was very specific—very beautiful, melodious. So, I dropped back down into the water and looked around. No dolphins, but right behind me was Scot and Edith, more of the regular dolphin swim crowd at this bay. They swim with the dolphins all the time and the dolphins love them. Edith sings beautiful songs to them and Scot plays "chase your tail" and "pass the leaf" for as long as the dolphins want to play. Scot also blows huge water rings that look like smoke rings made out of an air bubble. He blows them large enough for the dolphins to swim through, but only Scot has swam through them so far. (I have seen the dolphins blow big bubble rings and swim through them recently.) One day when Scot and Elizabeth were near, the dolphins made a beautiful tone I had never before heard them make. A few days later they repeated the tone when I was swimming with Elizabeth. After this happened a few more times, I realized that the dolphins (I believe), actually had a beautiful name or tone for Elizabeth. From that moment on, I noticed that whenever the dolphins sounded that particular tone, Elizabeth was approaching me, usually from behind.

Another example would be the day the dolphins began almost frantically making the tone for Helen when I was starting to get in my boat. She is a sweet little dolphin human if ever there was one. I noticed her in the middle of the pod for a couple of years before she ever actually spoke to me. A great photographer, she uses her healing touch on Montessori students she teaches too. I did not believe the dolphins could be correct in sounding her tone, as I was very, very far out to sea in my kayak, much further out than Helen should have been swimming. The dolphins were insistent in sounding her tone, so I took a look around. There she was a few feet away.

"Hey, girl, what you doing way out here?" I called to her.

Looking up, rather groggy with dolphin trance, she seemed surprised to see me. Turning her attention to shore, her face registered real surprise. "Oh, wow. I had no idea I was so far out. I was just following the dolphins. Can I catch a ride back in your Kayak?" She was not the first or the last to ride back to shore in my "dolphin swimmer's rescue boat." The dolphins made sure she got back to shore that day. Since then, I have learned quite a bit about tones with the dolphins. They have specific tones for several of the regular swimmers who come to the bay. As usual, when I began to study something specific with them, it is as if the dolphins know. The dolphins use these tones when I have not yet seen someone, and the tones match up with the same people consistently.

I have even seen how tones vibrate different organs in the body and how the organ responds by shifting shape somewhat. Eventually, through much practice, observation and research, I was able to match different tones to the bones they move. I now provide "home care kits" for my clients of crystal bowls, musically exact, which will assist bone movement to enhance their Craniosacral systems. For instance, the note "D" will release the sacral and pelvic bones, as well as the tissues around the pelvis—possible relief from menstrual cramps. The "A" note vibrates and loosens the forehead or frontal bone, which has shown anecdotal relief from stress, anxiety, depression, headaches. "A# " vibrates the pineal gland, balancing the pineal gland first, and then moving on to stimulate and balance the other organs in the endocrine system. It also vibrates the upper cranium from the inside out, providing release of bones and sutures as the sound expands the bones outward.

Again, I am not a doctor. I have extremely sensitive, well-honed skills of palpation, sound recognition, and visual assessment. Everyone has gifts. These are mine. I watch the movement of the bones, palpate them, and sometimes observe before and after x-rays, MRI's and CAT scans (with the assistance of professionals of course). I only relate my experiences and that of my clients. I do not diagnose or prescribe in any way. I present experiences simply to allow you, the reader, an opportunity to explore the concept that anything is possible.

Sound is considered the oldest form of healing by some. It was a predominant part of the early teachings of the Greeks, Chinese, East Indians, Tibetans, Egyptians, American Indians, Mayas, and the Aztecs. Pythagoras created the modern musical octave in an attempt to reveal the relationship between musical notes and the mathematical principles of the universe. I use that same scale to show which bones vibrate with which tones and show how to rebalance the Craniosacral system through sound. The dolphins taught me to use exact tone crystal bowls to accomplish what they can do using their sounds. The note "G# sharp" is excellent for releasing the occipital bones and the mandible. Clients suffering with Temporal Mandibular Joint (TMJ) malfunctions have found pain relief after the sound has vibrated the bones loose—so loose, that one needs to play a "B" note to allow the crown, which now seems tight, to release. Some bowls play one tone when you strike the side, another when you rotate the wand around the bowl. A very special bowl played "D," which was grounding for the client in addition to releasing the sacrum. When struck, it played "B," opening the crown and encouraging the flow from "D" (sacrum) to "B" (top of the head or crown), vibrating the spinal column up and down, between the two. "F" opens the heart physically and emotionally. "F# sharp" stimulates the thymus, which actually touches the thyroid in small children. It vibrates the mediastinum, so affects the heart too. While "A, A#, B, G# and D" encompass the bones of the Craniosacral system, stimulating the heart with "F" is vital to the treatment to help physically release emotions from the tissues.

The Greeks used sound for raising the consciousness of the individual to a sense of unity with the divine. When we create harmony, rather than dissonance, in our very bones, increased health is the benefit. If you strike a tuning fork to the tone of "middle C" next to a piano, and then gently run your fingers along the piano wires, you will find that middle C is vibrating. The same thing happens with specific bones in the body. I found which bones vibrate to which tones. I have also corresponded tones to organs. Thoughts and colors cause vibration as much as voices, musical instruments, and other sounds. We can accumulate sound "debris" as we go through life that results in stress and restrictions, eventually, even pain, in our joints and bones. Sound Therapy can release and balance the bones when used correctly. Although we work extensively with sound in water, air is the most common carrier of sound for most people. The motion of the vibrating origin is passed from one molecule of air to the next and the next, and so on. The human ear can pick up between 16 and 20,000 vibrations per second. The human body will then FEEL the pulsations even though they are not heard—which must have been what was happening to me on this ride.

Suddenly, I see the sign for Makena Landing flash by.

"Stop, turn around. You missed Makena Landing," I call out.

"I did not know we were going there," my husband said with just a bit of sarcasm.

We went to the next turn and circled back. Coming down a hill, you could see the bay. A boat was pulled up to the landing; a much bigger boat than could actually launch from there. The boat was not all the way to the launch. We could see as we drove closer. There were twenty or more people lined up from the shore through the ocean, passing green bags down the line until it reached the boat; Men, women, children, mostly Hawaiian. Something pulled me to them. We parked just above and watched as one after another the green garbage bags were passed hand-to-hand along the waiting line into the boat. I began to cry softly. My heart was stretching. It almost hurt in some way and I cried more as I tried to resist the stretching and pulling in my heart. I could feel an ancient way of life, a culture. I could not stop crying. Where were they going? I could feel their mission—that they were helping someone or something. Could they be going to Molokai to the old leper colony? I was guessing now. No, that was not it. To Kahoolawe? I just could not stop crying. The last bag was in the boat. Now the teenagers started to climb aboard. The boat was loaded until it was fuller than you could have believed. Everyone was so silent and so peaceful. Others waited patiently, sitting on the beach. Still, I could not stop crying.

One woman came up the hill behind us, passing on to an old pickup truck. I walked over to her. "Hi. Sorry to bother you. I would not usually just walk over and ask someone what they are doing, but, whatever it is, it makes me cry. I feel so much love."

(I cry now as I write this). First, she appeared somewhat shocked and taken aback. Then, it was as if she physically reached through my tears to me. She held out her hand and took mine, and told me her name.

"We are the Ohana to Protect Kaho'olawe. We are going there to reclaim the land, plant, care for it."

"What you are doing is very beautiful," I told her, still

holding her hand and crying, I think.

"Thank you."

Many years of love, praying, working, and dying went into the heart and soul of this group, I knew from stories over the years. Something had called me to witness them this morning. Something had struck at the very structure of my heart and stretched it open. Perhaps there are invisible tones, vibrations, set in motion through the reality that touches us, created by the powerful emotions we express as we experience our lives. It was this experience that so touched me, I had finally started to listen to what the dolphins wanted to teach me about sound in relation to vibration. The problem had been that they were requesting that I acquire multiple crystal bowls—not an inexpensive move. It had also come to the point where, when I did not insist that people bring crystal bowls on my latest experiential to Bimini, the dolphins refused to talk to me about it anymore, with one exception. They would say, "Swim. Just swim."

Great. So, I spent a few thousand dollars (that is each), on the best bowls available, (Poor service from the company advertising; excellent service, unfortunately.). Not only did the dolphins speak to me again, they blew me away with how much they could increase perception in general, with their training. The treatments are unreal. I go into detail on my DVD, "An Introduction to AquaCranial and Craniosacral Therapies Amplified with Crystal Bowls." I use the bowls in my "Moving Bones with Tones" classes and on the accompanying DVD.

The dolphins began teaching us to "hear color." The bowls became tools for accelerating the releases in the cranial sacral system, the skeletal system, tissues, and muscles, combining tones and the alchemy of metals and minerals. Craniosacral and AquaCranial Therapy disorganize the electrical system so that it can reorganize in a more coherent manner. By adding the use of a tool that reorganizes the bioelectrical field through the use of pure tones, a whole world of possibilities emerges. Again, the dolphins have shown us a way to do what they do—

this time, using sound.

***The hassles I encountered while attempting to acquire high quality bowls, inspired me to offer Crystal Bowls for sale. Visit our website for more information. www.aquacranial.com

CHAPTER 9
CETACEAN HEALING

"Marine mammals receive and transmit sound signals capable of affecting the genetic double helix, and using natural biotechnology, dolphins may heal humans swimming near them sonogenetically."

A startling report by Dr. Michael Hyson explains how the dolphin's acoustic and electromagnetic effects on the body through DNA may best explain remarkable healings experienced with the dolphins. Multitudes of people pass across my therapy table with any number of skills and professions. I learn many things from them. Light conversation is relaxing during the initial phase of Craniosacral Therapy. Of course, with AquaCranial, there is little conversation. We do soft research dealing with frequency-mediated, psycho-physiological responses in biological systems. Our focus is the affect of dolphin and whale ultrasonic frequencies on brain hormone release and its subsequent effect on the Craniosacral system of the body and emotional release.

Our secondary focus is the electromagnetic field-to-field effect. When a client mentioned he was a brain research doctor, I immediately ran my pet theory past him. I believe that in the case of depressed persons, the dolphins' sonar the limbic portion of the brain. When the resulting ecstasy starts to leave and the letdown of bliss happens, in many cases, the return to a "normal" emotional state is much less depressed than before the sonar blast from the dolphin to the brain. It is similar to the way a tight muscle, when stretched correctly, will return to a less restricted motion. After a thoughtful moment, the brain re-search doctor said slowly, "Well, assuming the dolphin could actually target the limbic portion of the brain to sonar it, your theory could be possible."

Ultrasonic frequencies used in hospitals typically are in the range of 80mW/cm2 for diagnostic purposes to 2mW/cm2 for treatment of traumatic injuries. Dolphins produce echolocation sound or ultrasonic vibratory sound frequencies at intensities of 8.3mW/cm2. This means dolphins naturally produce an ultra-sonic frequency that is four times the frequency used for thera-peutic purposes in clinics and hospitals. Add to that the fact that dolphin ultrasound is delivered through water, which is 60 times more efficient than air as a medium for sound transfer-ence!

I was sure there were physiological responses with our dol-phin/human interactions, so checked other things as well. My heart is not the best; my pulse is usually 85 to 105 resting. I measured it by machine approximately three times a week over the past several years. Only after swimming with dolphins does it drop to 65. Even if I swim an equivalent time without dol-phins, my pulse will not drop as low afterwards. The energetic field of a person changes dramatically after swimming with dolphins. I can see it even if I have no idea that the person just came from swimming with the dolphins. I will be in town, see a glowing person walk by and say, "Hey, you just swam with dolphins, didn't you?"

The answer is always "Yes."

I can treat 30 babies in clinic and ask only one mama, "This baby has been with dolphins, yes?"

The answer is always "Yes."

It will also be the only baby of the 30 that was in the water with dolphins. Many people study the energetic effects of swimming with dolphins. Recent research has shown that sig-nificant improvements in cognitive responses occurred in men-tally retarded children subjected to dolphin interaction. Brain wave measurements have also been shown to change significantly in subjects exposed to dolphin interactions. The usefulness of dolphins in biomedical engineering research has recently been investigated and modern studies of cetacean acoustic transmissions are now accomplished using digital signal processing analysis and neural networks. There is even a group of doctors working to create a pill that makes you feel like you do when you swim with dolphins. There is no doubt in my mind that swimming with dolphins reduces the stress hormones in the body. I am sure someone else will figure out all the details of how and why.

The electromagnetic component of the human energy field can be detected with special instruments. It is through manipulation of the Craniosacral system with electromagnetic energy that the dolphins have been teaching me how to heal. I get into this with the advanced training and research trips we do with AquaCranial. The reduction in tissue, muscle, and emotional distress is nearly immediate in treatment. It is possible that electromagnetic releases influence the energy field to the point that unhealthy or dysfunctional physical, emotional, and psychological states of being or patterns will diminish or disappear. This has been the case in clinical situations where patients are receiving a series of AquaCranial treatments. It would seem the dolphins have the capacity to alter human tissue with ultrasonic vibration. Their sounds have been observed to be different when they are in a healing mode than when they are in a play mode. They appear to modulate the frequency and location of their interaction.

There are many stories of tumors disappearing when patients swim with dolphins. Tumors are currently "dissolved" using ultrasound in hospitals. Not all tumors can be eliminated with ultrasound or sonar, in hospitals or swimming with dolphins. Nothing cures everything. Faith can sometimes be healing even when there is no "cure." Other stories exist of dolphins somehow letting a swimmer know that there was something wrong with a specific part of their body. Later examination will reveal a tumor or other problem where the dolphin repeatedly pushed against someone. A woman who works with birthing told me a story of swimming with a pregnant woman and dolphins. The dolphins continued to surround and sonar the pregnant woman over and over. Within hours after leaving the ocean, she went into labor, even though she was only seven and a half months pregnant. The baby came quickly. The cord was wrapped around the baby's neck more than once and the baby was blue. Even though the mother had no idea there was a problem, the doctors said it was a miracle she went into labor and delivered when she did. The baby would not have lived much longer the way things were.

A new and exciting branch of medicine is psychoneurological immunology. It proposes, in a nutshell, that some of our immune systems are mediated by psychological factors. It is in this vein that we have some of our most thought-provoking discoveries. While our research is mainly qualitative, some measurement and statistical analysis is done as well. Research tools include (but are not limited to): pre- and post-interview sessions, physiological tests and observations, brainwave analysis, spinal analysis, videotapes of treatments, before and after client photos, questionnaires, and statistical analysis. The purpose of this book is to introduce you to the work we do at Cetacea Bleu and entertain you with a few dolphin stories. If we can educate you a bit and stretch your mind, there is a therapist near you who can loosen your skull to accommodate.

I swim with whales and dolphins. I "feel" them. I duplicate the feeling with my electromagnetic field. I then use my field to influence and adjust someone else's field the way I have observed the cetaceans doing it. The whales told me they were going to teach us "holographic listening," which I now believe is being conscious and listening with our field as well as the rest of our senses. It felt like "listening" with my skin and with a part of me that extended inches off my body. I practice going through the different states radiated by the whales. I literally connect my field to theirs and move wherever they take me in consciousness. I have had children and young adults make comments about the whales "touching" them. They have even related that: "Rebecca is in the whale touching me!"

I check the amplitude, frequency, and strength of the Craniosacral systems of participants, as well as any physical restrictions or emotional blockages prior to their coming into contact with the whales or dolphins. I recheck them after their dolphin and whale encounters. When someone has been specifically targeted by the cetaceans, the difference in the cranial field is especially dramatic. While thousands of table and AquaCranial treatments have shown the water treatments to be about three times deeper and more effective than table treatments, the whale touch is a hundred times greater. In the early days of my training with the whales, I would watch 150 tourists "fall asleep" in the middle of an afternoon Whale Watch. Excitedly watching the mammoth creatures breach above the waves, talking to each other, etc., then suddenly, 90% of the boat gone, knocked out. I always found it interesting that the most likely to remain awake were infants and toddlers who would give me the "Hey, you feel it too" look. The moment I would feel the whales turn off their bio field, everyone on the boat would wake up all at once, and start talking away. They seemed unaware of the experience in most cases.

I have also been in the middle of a conversation with someone on the boat who is complaining they don't like their life, their job sucks, the weather is too cloudy, and then, WHAM! I feel the whale's bio field hit. Suddenly, the person calmly, and in a rather light and airy manner, looks around and starts making statements like, "Wow! It is so beautiful here, have you ever seen such incredibly blue water? Oh my, this is an awesome place. I love my life."

When I worked doing treatments in a cabana on a deck overlooking the ocean at Huloopoe' Bay on Lanai at the Manele Bay Hotel, a mama and whale baby were there daily for three months. Someone would lie down on the table. Within minutes, mama whale would turn on her bio field and the guest would pass out. I could have walked away at that moment, returned an hour later, and no one would have noticed. People would wake up, look at me with a weird look, and say, "What the heck just happened?"

The kids get it. They talked me into going to Oahu to testify in front of the Navy. It has been proven that low frequency sound testing by the Navy was hurting the whales. The hearing was to determine if the Navy should be granted a permit to kill a certain number of whales per year so that their testing could continue. Of course, they got the permit, we have "acceptable" human casualty numbers for the military, and we can certainly accept whale casualties. The children thought perhaps if people understood how much the whales helped to heal us, someone may rethink hurting and killing them. I spoke for the keiki. No matter what else happens, the records show that they stood up and said "NO."

I speak for the cetaceans now. They speak to me in a variety of very specific ways. For instance, it was the dolphins that said they wanted to work with me on Lanai and that I would be given a room at the Manele Bay Hotel. I was given a great $300 to $500 a night room and free ferry tickets for close to a year. I had to do massage in the spa, but I had flexibility in setting my schedule AND they paid me. After I started working there, the spa added a deck for massage on the cliffs overlooking the ocean. Inside the cabana, guests would clap and laugh, as dolphins, sometimes as many as three at a time, would leap out of the ocean, spinning in front us at the edge of the cliff. These dolphins choreographed spins 15-feet high and more! It was like Sea World, only these dolphins were not trained. They created the show just because they wanted to in that moment. Then they were truly free to swim off and live the way they chose.

I will have to write an entire book on just the Lanai dolphin experiences. Amazing healing was happening on the table, when I incorporated what I learned from the dolphins into table Craniosacral treatments. A 45-year-old woman had a predominant curve in her chin. Her chin curved in a 90-degree angle towards her ear, so that the bottom of her face curved into a C shape. After several surgeries, she was still wearing braces and nothing seemed to help. The damage had come from forceps at birth. When she arrived for her second treatment, she laughed and was simply amazed.

"Rebecca," she said, "I put on my sunglasses and my eyebrows are in a different place on my face!"

By the third treatment, her face was symmetrical. I have doctors and nurses that want to draw lines from bone to bone to see if the bones actually move or just feel like it. Draw lines, x-ray before and after, I do not care. The bones move. One day, the dolphins said, "Call the Four Seasons, it is time for you to work there."

I picked up the phone and started dialing.

"What are you doing?" my husband asked.

"Calling the Seasons for a job," I replied.

"Did they have an ad in the paper?" he asked.

"No, it is just time."

I left a voicemail message for the spa director. The next day the principle therapist called. I had a nametag and was working 24-hours later. They had 40 therapists doing what was considered the best job on an island with 4000 licensed therapists. It was not usually that easy to get on at the Seasons, but the dolphins have a plan. During a very dead time at work, the dolphins informed me they wanted me to go to Bimini and go out with Knowdla.

"What is Knowdla and where is Bimini?" I asked.

Checking the internet for Knowdla and Bimini, I found that Bimini is an island in the Bahamas, and Bill and Knowdla O'Keefe have a dive shop and, you guessed it, dolphin trips. Having zero money, I just laughed at the dolphins.

"Money?" they said. "That's it?"

Several thousand dollars in unexpected treatments (during the off season) came in over the next couple of weeks.

"Is that enough?" the dolphins wanted to know.

So, I went on my first trip to Bimini and the healing hole. The soft, gentle pink-bellied, Spotted dolphins have much to show in the turquoise waters, and much of Atlantis to tell—or so they say. They are by far the gentlest of the dolphins—SO sweet. They swim right up about two inches from your nose and just look into your eyes. They can also be the most hyper of the dolphins, adding extra excitement to the encounter. On a subsequent trip to Bimini, I had a very difficult woman in the group and an even more difficult situation. After swimming with the Spotted dolphins for a week in the relaxing environment of this little Third World island, the group from Hades arrived. Someone in town stated that they could usually tell what a group was like by the leader of the group, and the leader of this group was a bitch. In fact, the bitch was actually the wife of the group leader—not the leader himself. It was a complicated situation. She wanted a vacation with her husband. She believed he was too cheap to give it to her, so had set up this pseudo-workshop, and she was pissed. He claimed it was a vacation, not a workshop, and these people had just joined the vacation. Of course, it was those people who paid a price that enabled the guru, his wife, his two daughters, the wife's son and daughter in law, to all have their "vacation" paid.

I already had some previous issues with the wife, and I had not really wanted to take this group. My husband was sure she would ruin things, as was her nature at the time, and had asked me to not do it in the first place. The guru and I were old friends, and he convinced me it would be fun—and his wife would behave. The day before they landed on the island, I suddenly went from dolphin blissful to apprehensive. Something not-so-good was coming. The first day, the group arrived late; everyone was scattered. They had made their own reservations for rooms in Miami and were bounced to another hotel when theirs was overbooked. The twenty-minute flight to Bimini did not happen as the plane broke down. They were bussed to Fort Lauderdale, where the group was split onto two different planes.

Bimini is actually two islands and they were flown to the other island and then had to be ferried over to us. The twenty-minute flight took four hours and we were still missing half the group. The wife wanted to leave the ones who had not arrived yet behind. This was to set the pace for discontent on her part. We managed to get everyone onto the boats anyway. Being on the ocean has a tendency to calm people, and this group was already exhausted. Soon, the dolphins came. We all jumped in for an exciting swim, everyone thrilled to be with the dolphins so quickly. As the sun was setting, we swam slowly back to the boat. The darkening sky, streaked with brilliant reds and corals, followed us back to shore and our hotels. The next morning began badly. I will not get into personal details, but when the dolphins came flying towards the boat, it was if they suddenly hit an invisible wall and stopped. They then took off and we saw no more dolphins on that trip. When we all discussed it in later days, many mentioned this incident. Amid continuing dissatisfaction in the group that the guru was not doing anything (in his mind he was on vacation, of course), his wife was spreading venom through the small town. Not only did I have multiple complaints from trip participants about the guru's lack of participation, but town's people were coming to me with horror stories. It came down to a real shouting match.

One of the actors on the trip, who was the sole witness, said it seemed like a normal L.A. business meeting to him. I was in over my head, so I walked out to appeal to the dolphins. I told them that if they wanted me to keep working for them, I needed some help this time. It would be the last time that I accommodated a group with no real focus. Future research trips would be detailed by us not left to someone else, no matter who they might be. My hands were tied. I could not do my own thing and the group leader was doing nothing with the group he had booked.

An hour or so later, we were sailing across the shallow reef about 45 minutes from shore. I was hanging over the very front of the boat when the first three Bottlenose' shot under me.

There was no doubt in my mind, I knew these were my dolphins, come to help me. The energy of the Bottlenose dolphins is much stronger and can handle energies that are more disharmonic. Knowdla was explaining to us that Bottlenose occasionally buzzed the boat, but never stayed more than a few minutes. We should go find some Spotted dolphins to swim with, as the Bottlenose would not swim with us. She suddenly interrupted herself, screaming and pointing excitedly. There were dolphins leaping and jumping in the air, coming at the boat from three directions. It was if they had triangulated the boat and were flying at us. The Bottlenose dolphins do not travel in large pods like the spinners. In no time, there were 13 Bottlenose' lined across the front of the boat under my feet. By now, everyone was screaming and jumping, all thoughts but the dolphins forgotten.

"Never have I ever seen so many Bottlenose together," Knowdla exploded.

Neither had I. "Stop the boat," I called out to Knowdla. "We need to get in the water with them."

Knowdla slowed, but did not stop the boat. "They will not stay. They do not swim with people here, only the Spotted dolphins swim with people," she repeated.

"Jeez Knowdla, you say the dolphins do things with us they do not usually do. I have worked on you, on your kids..." I began in protest.

"You are right," she said, quickly shutting off the boat.

We all got in the water. The dolphins did not leave; they swam all around us. The energy shift was tangible; everyone let go of stress and strife. After a while, their work done, the Bottlenose dolphins left. We took a short ride in the boat before being surrounded by Spotted dolphins. Our energy shift had softened every one enough to attract the pink-bellied beauties, so we jumped in and swam with them for a while. There were several amazing stories on that trip. My favorite is about a ten-year-old boy with autism. He had jumped out of his seat when I decompressed his cranium the first day.

"Whoa!" he yelled out, as energy shot out of his head as fast as he jumped.

He had let me do several decompressions on his body while he sat perfectly still. Medial decompression of the cranial vault was the only thing that had been so intense. The next day, knocked out by the dolphins and therapy, he skipped the boat trip. Even in his sleep, I had to decompress the cranial vault a thousand times slower than the rest of his body. The trip had been disconcerting coming to the island, so he was worse than normal on arrival—very abusive, repetitive, and not coherent at all. On the third day in the healing hole, he had an excellent treatment and we had a nice talk—the first. He told me of how he dressed and what he ate. He had not said two consecutive words to me before now. Then he said, "Do you know why you do not go in the healing hole?"

"No why?" I asked, amazed he was so coherent.

"Because the alligators will get you!" he laughed, jumping in my arms and tickling me.

It was on his last day with the dolphins, with everyone so excited over first, the Bottlenose, and then, the Spotted dolphins that his mother swam over to me. The dolphins were cruising all around Danny in his life ring.

"I wish he could actually see the whole dolphin instead of just fins," his mother said wistfully.

We had him in the ocean surrounded by dolphins in his swim ring, but it was not possible for him to use a mask and snorkel. For the second time on this trip, I implored the dolphins for a bit more help. Immediately, two dolphins leaped out of the water and flew past Danny's head; the baby dolphin inches from his face. Danny watched them until he almost flipped over backwards in his float ring. His face lit up with that "I have been touched by a dolphin" beam. His mother joyfully said, "I think he saw them. They were right there. Look at him."

Danny did not quit smiling. He very clearly told me more of his special stories. People who saw him that night did not realize he had any challenges. He seemed like an average, healthy, boy. I am not saying he was cured, by any means. It was quite an experience for him, however. The children teach me so much. My little German client, Sylvy, received treatments for six months. She went through two trainings for practitioners before her third birthday. She would tell people she was Rebecca and it was now time for their treatment. Tiny, little, Sylvy would move their heads around, look at them seriously, and say, "You are VERY brave."

Obviously, to her, it took bravery to go through treatments, and I would take this into consideration when treating adult clients too. She knew no English, I knew no German. We both learned. She learned to order me around in German, and I learned to understand her. Sylvy had great anger for such a tiny girl. She bit people—hard! She was very aggressive. That aggressiveness and biting were the first to lighten up after she began treatments. I did mouth work from outside; there was no way she was letting me work inside her mouth. Until then, every child I ever treated allowed me to do what I wanted after the first or second treatment, even the difficult ones. Not so with Sylvy. I was lucky to get to touch her hand in the beginning. We made a game. She in her swim floaty, with Mom near by.

"Hund," I would say in a slow, exaggerated way.

"Hand," she would repeat.

Later she would let me hold out her tiny hand, stretched wide. I would work up from there, adjusting the arm, the thoracic area, into the cervical bones, and eventually into the facial bones. After time, I could hold her feet. We would pretend she was the truck and I, the driver. While pushing her around the ocean by her legs, with her in her swimmy, I would adjust upwards. Legs, hips, pelvic bones, up the spinal column, into the thoracic area. The first changes her parents noticed were that she was not nearly as aggressive and did not bite people often, if at all. They could also tell that her mouth closed completely differently when she ate. This convinced her parents to continue her therapy. Sylvy's anger was still present. So much anger for a two-and-a-half-year-old. Her parents had no idea what the cause.

As Sylvy would allow me to touch her more, I began to release her deeper. The swim trainer was a Godsend. It was her mother that worked miracles here on earth. She would distract Sylvy with stories. Long involved stories with Stephanie leaping, diving, and changing her voice, the tempo of it sweeping Sylvy away. She would become so enthralled with the stories that I could treat away without her paying me any attention. The stories were in German. I understood dolphins, Rebecca, Sylvy, and of course, dive deeper. Even I could not help but be mesmerized by Stephanie, her bright brown eyes flashing in her exotically beautiful face; the brilliant blue ocean lit with golden rays of the sun reflecting around her. Even the billowing white clouds in both the sky and reflecting off the ocean's surface seemed to be created to be her backdrop. Sylvy did best with three appointments a week. When we cut back to one, she did not do nearly as well.

"I know, she gets a treatment, she has a meltdown and cries for awhile, and then she sleeps very well. Then, she is much better than before the treatment. I know the drill by now," Stephanie would say.

She brought Sylvy to Hawaii looking to find a cure for her before Sylvy knew there was anything wrong with her. Sylvy's left hand and arm were frozen, pulled upwards and into her body like a broken wing held close. She had cerebral palsy. Over time, she could stretch out her arm and build sand castles with her hand. When she had more emotional days, you could see her still draw her arm into her, somewhat. Eventually, with enough treatment, I believe it is possible that her body will "figure it out" and not need the continuing treatments. Her left leg loosened considerably, but by this time, she was three years old and holding it up had become a habit. Putting her in a splint (her doctor) for a bit helped retrain Sylvy and kept her muscles from atrophying. It was months of dolphins, ocean side treatments, and therapy in the ocean itself, before I discovered a possible cause for her anger. She had still not let me inside of her mouth for treatments.

Sylvy was like many children with traumatic conditions. She was not much into my touching her—but, in the kayak, everything changes. Like many children before her, Sylvy completely relaxed in my lap and let me treat her, moving cranial bones and decompressing tissues while she contentedly melted back into me. She would become very quiet and eventually sleep. Ty would paddle us along, dolphins joining us some days, turtles and whales cruising our kayak other times; her parents, in the kayak beside us. We would cruise along the Maui coastline. Sometimes, the whales would call to us and we would paddle out a mile or two. Hooking the kayaks together, laying aside our paddles, we would float along with the wind and currents. Whales would come along side and sing beautiful songs to us. When the whales first told me to bring the children out to them, I was a definite novice. My first year kayaking the open ocean, I was told to go to a specific place, for weeks before our kayaks arrived. When people would ask where we planned to kayak out, they would laugh, stare at me, or try to convince me I should go to the places everyone else went for whales. Mile Marker 14, Makena Landing, they would say, trying to convince me that "everyone" went out the same places. No one went where I planned to go.

Nevertheless, we got our kayaks, loaded them up with babies and parents and went out two miles off a beach no one else was departing anywhere near. We hooked the four kayaks together in a "play pen" and played with the babies, treating them in the deep blue. We did this every day for three months, in the same place that first year. Every day, the same mama whale brought her new baby to join us. Many, many, other whales came to join our floating playpen. We knew the same mama came everyday by her markings. I thought that perhaps they felt that since we brought our babies, it was cool to bring their babies.

The second year, two mama whales, two newborns, and a yearling joined us—every day for three months. A whale's tale is like fingerprints. No two are alike, so it is easy to identify them. Sylvy would be with us when the mama whale picked up her newborn and carried it to the front of my kayak. A couple of weeks before they returned to Germany, I was speaking with Sylvy's father.

"Come on, Dimitry, think." I was pushing hard; they were leaving in a week or so. I had asked repeatedly with no results but… "Look, someone was really angry when this child was born. It is not her anger. She picked it up from someone. Maybe the nurse dropped something and the doctor got angry and yelled at her. Think hard."

Dimitry screwed his face into concentration then shook his head.

"No, the doctor was not angry. Only me," he suddenly shot out, angry now. "It was a double bullet. First, she is pregnant. Then, it is a stupid girl," he continued with force. "I am pretty much over it now though," he said, as if he suddenly realized it; no anger in his voice now.

I was amazed. I had asked the same question for months. Apparently, he was not ready to "release" the information or the energy surrounding it until now. Sylvy fell asleep as we spoke. I gently brushed her cheek. In her sleep, for the first time, she let me work inside her mouth. Dr. Upledger refers to the mouth as "the avenue of expression." Much tension in everyone's body eventually leads back to the mouth. With the anger expressed and thus, released from her father, it was easy for little Sylvy to let it go and allow me to finally release the inside bones of her mouth.

The whales also use sonar. Oh to be kissed by a whale. It only happens if they choose it, coming like a torpedo, possibly even from a mile or more out. Every time, I have seen the force hit inside the area of the heart and lungs, imploding from there outward. At that point, the person so blessed as to be sonared by the whale, many times, bursts into tears and starts shaking all over. Physically stress is relieved from the tissues, fascia, and viscera in a way I cannot even imagine happening by any other means. The heart seems to open.

"It was like ten years of therapy," one shaken woman told me gratefully. After laughing, crying and babbling. She suddenly looked at me. "Don't worry," she said. "I won't tell anyone."

I laughed. "Are you kidding? You are going to be in my book! You have just been kissed by a whale."

The lungs are open and breathing is, at the very least, ten times deeper. I have seen restrictions let go in an instant that could take a 100 treatments to release on the table. Do not bother to call and make an appointment for this one. I cannot get the whales to do it any way. Sometimes, it just happens. Like a miracle at Lourdes. Speaking of odd... after several years of treatments, something new occurred a couple of years ago. We offered to give our boat captain, Willy, a treatment during deep-water training. He had never before experienced AquaCranial Therapy. I stayed onboard to watch the boat and to videotape. The other students jumped out of the boat, put on their float rings, and surrounded Willy. They gave him an air pillow for his head and he stretched out on the world's biggest waterbed—the ocean. Everything was going fine for the first ten minutes. Then out of nowhere, a whale appeared underneath the group and sonared Willy right through his heart. It was magnetic, like a pole coming out of the ocean, spearing straight through him. His entire body began to shake. He started to sit up at the same time saying, "I don't think I can do this."

Four therapists simultaneously said, "Lay down Willy," while pushing him flat with their hands.

Then Willy began to spin like the needle on a compass, with Willy the needle and the flat surface of the ocean the compass. He spun so quickly that he literally threw one therapist completely off his body. Seventeen very quick times, he spun around, before slowing to a stop. The therapists finished the treatment and helped Willy into the boat. He was not speaking; just looked at me out of the corner of his eye with 'that' look. The therapists laid him down on the boat, covered him up, and then jumped right back into the water.

"I want to do that!" exclaimed Lynnette, a new trainee. She lay down and put the pillow under her head. "Do me now!"

"Okay," I said, "but no matter what happens, do not stop treating her. Just keep going."

Later, they would remind me of that statement when I noticed in the video that she tried to get up three or four times, but they kept her down.

"What were you doing?" I asked.

"She wanted up when the whales came to us, but you told us not to stop no matter what!"

She also began spinning in the same way. You had to get into the vortex with her to keep up. Later, small children would spin fast enough to throw off several full-grown adults. The water can be turbulent or flat as glass. You can actually see the spinning vortex in the center of the still water in photos and videos. After the first season, this spinning began to happen in near-shore treatments—no longer just in deep water. The whales do not have to be anywhere near for it to happen. Whales do come to us. We do not move when it happens, just observe or get back in the boat, if we happen to be in the water. We have observed the whales form three rings, each farther from us, yet still revolving around us, when we do deep-water treatments. Other people not associated with our group have noticed and commented on the same thing, the whales encircling us. Many other people have noticed that it is the whales, indeed, who approach us, and not the other way around.

In Hawaii, I always follow the rules, although, sometimes, the whales do not. Of course, the whales interacted with people in the islands long before the rules to "not harass the whales" were established. We would never harass whales. Sometimes, the whales would come up behind our boats, when someone was chasing them in a kayak, or even motorboat. The little children would stand up in the kayaks and shout out to them, "Back off. Do not harass the whales."

It is illegal to approach within 100-yards of the whales. I will stay back 150, if she is nursing and wants the space. When they come five feet under my kayak and start singing, it is like sitting inside of giant stereo speakers. It is referred to as "a whale mugging" when they come that close.

You have to sit still and not move until the whales leave. I have no problem "not moving."

CHAPTER 10
WHAT CONSTITUTES NATURAL BEHAV-IOR?

An Australian Aboriginal Tribe included the following in their version of the Creation of Earth... "The dolphins never forgot that all these 'two-legged' humans on land are their cousins and that is why nowadays the dolphins come to find their human relatives, and play with them as they did in the dreamtime."

Aristotle was a biologist as well as a philosopher. Studying dolphins, he thought that dolphins were interested in getting closer to us. He wrote about the dolphin's intelligence, which he thought to be as great as human intelligence, although of a different kind. The earliest signs we have of contact between dolphins and humans are recorded in drawings in Stone Age caves in Norway and South Africa. In the late 1700's, La Parouse, a French explorer, wrote in his journal that the Hawaiians swam out to his boat as easily as seals and the creatures in the sea. That was in the same bay where dolphins swim with us today. Romans, Polynesians, and Americans all write about the mysterious rescue of shipwreck victims. Who was not moved by the story little Elian told of his being surrounded by dolphins that protected him from sharks on his flight from Cuba?

"Sometimes, I was so tired I could no longer hold on and would slip down into the water. The dolphins would push me back up into the life ring, keeping my head above the water. They never left me," he said.

A man scuba diving in front of the Grand Wailea Hotel on

Maui during the Winter of 2001, saw a 16-foot tiger shark swimming very quickly straight towards him and his 14-year-old son. Suddenly, a large Bottlenose dolphin rammed the shark. The dolphin then placed himself between the shark and the diver with his son, escorting them to shore.

Fishermen say dolphins help them fish. The Navy uses dolphins for very sophisticated sonar and echolocation programs, e.g., finding bombs. A university of Hawaii psychologist teaches dolphins sign language, 900 signs, in an experiment proving that dolphins understand syntax. (Get the green ball under the third chair on the left, for example). In fact, dolphins have also been found to understand an artificial language. Dolphins are able to spontaneously mimic sounds. They have shown stages of vocal learning seen only in humans and in some birds, and they have unique whistles to identify themselves. This individual identity is unusual in animals other than humans. Dolphins have more DNA in common with humans than do humans with any other land mammal. Could there be something to the Australian "Creation myth's" claim that we are indeed relatives? Did our ancestors know something we have forgotten?

Bonds form between individual dolphins that last a lifetime. They have been observed physically supporting sick or dying pod members. The Bedouins call the dolphins ABU SALAM, which means, father of peace. In ancient Greek myths, dolphins are the messengers of the god Apollo. There are myths and legends about dolphins in old Greece and old India, by the Dogon tribe in Mali, in stories of the Aborigines, and the Kwakiuti Indians. Plutarch reports the story of a man named Korianos from the Isle of Pharos. He once convinced fishermen, who had captured a pod of dolphins, to set them free. Years later, his boat sank close to the coast and all the people died—except Korianos. He was saved by the dolphins that he once saved. The day Korianos died, the dolphins showed up again. They came close to the shore and waited there until his body was burned and the ceremony completed.

Dr. John Lilly, who provided extensive research on dolphins, performed the following experiments.

Using a mind probe set in the brain, which when stimulated with an electrical current, gave the dolphin a rewarding sensation, Dr. Lilly set up a switch where Dolphin #6 could reward himself by pushing a lever. "While assembling it, I noticed that the dolphin was closely watching what I was doing. Almost before I could finish assembling and placing the rods necessary to push the switch (which was out of the water above the animal), the dolphin started pushing on the rod. By the time the switch was connected to the rest of the apparatus, he had learned the proper way to push it." Dr. Lilly used the same technique on monkeys, who he said usually took about 100 random tries before even learning to push the button.

Dr. Lilly was attempting to make Dolphin #8 whistle a burst of a given pitch, duration, and intensity in order to obtain a reward. The dolphin caught on quickly. Every time he whistled, his blowhole would move and a whistle would be emitted. Then, Dr. Lilly noticed that the dolphin had added a new rule to the game. He was raising the pitch of each subsequent whistle. Suddenly, the blowhole twitched, but no sound. No sound—no reward. Dolphin #8 emitted two more supersonic twitches and the third was audible.

From that time on, he did not go out of Dr. Lilly's acoustic range. The dolphin had determined what Dr. Lilly's hearing range was and stayed within it. Dr. Lilly taught us much. I hope we remember—as I do not agree with dolphin captivity.

Dolphin #8 died shortly after this session. I personally have never cut, captured, embedded transmitters in cetaceans, or otherwise tagged, endangered, or harassed any marine mammal in the pursuit of cetacean therapy education. In return, the dolphins have taught me how to heal using some of the ways that the dolphins heal. The time has come for me to speak up personally for my distant relatives, the dolphins, with whom I have bonded for over two decades. The impetus for my finally speaking came from a little girl and a federal officer. La Perouse Bay was virtually empty except for the dolphins, fishermen, Hawaiians, and a handful of die-hard swimmers, just a few years ago. For many years,, it was kapu or forbidden to haoles or white man. It was only for the Hawaiians. It took years before I would go out there. Even though I knew nothing of the kapu, I could feel it. The ancestors eventually called me down there. They always speak to me in Hawaiian, and I have to have it translated or use a book to do it myself. I am not Hawaiian. Maybe they knew I would help Hawaiian babies too, someday. Or perhaps they knew I would eventually have a grandbaby of Hawaiian ancestry. Today, the Hawaiians want the haoles gone from the area. It is sacred they say. Perhaps they do not see that sacred land calls to people of all races.

There is a sacred spring high on Mount Shasta in California. The Indians go there for ceremony. Many, many times, the mountain called me for these ceremonies. I would drive for hours or fly from the islands; wherever I was, I would go. Eventually, one of the Indians, in their speech during the ceremony, mentioned that while many were called by their Indian family, others had been called by the mountain. I have spent enough time at La Parouse in the last decade to see it call many people from many cultures around the world to come to the sacred ground. One night as I walked on lava rocks uncovered by the very low tide, the land spoke to me.

"This is sacred ground."

"Okay," I said, "but all land is sacred. What are you trying to tell me?"

"This land is purified. God said this land would remain under water for 10,000 years, then it would rise again. This land is purified."

Now, I do not know if we are talking about a rise in consciousness, actual land rising, or what. I do know that approximately 10,000 years ago Molikini Crater formed from some kind of earth upheaval, which I find kind of interesting. Today, the Feds are there writing tickets. Do not get me wrong—I am first in line to protect the resource. However, what is really happening here? When the ticket writing starts for harassing the dolphins, the bay clears of people. And many times, dolphins, as well. Here is where it gets interesting. I pointed out to our federal officer that the dolphins seemed to seek out human interaction. He said, indeed, that was obvious. It was also what made it illegal, as it is unnatural for dolphins to want to be around humans.

Disturbing the natural actions and habits of the dolphins is illegal. As a matter of fact, as humans, we really do not have the right to even be in the water—water not being a natural environment for humans. That is, 72% to 90% of the planet (depending on which statistics you use), humans do not "naturally" belong on, according to his theory. He further stated that "I am only one person." All kayakers, dolphin lovers, cetacean therapists, etc., are in the minority, and the big machines of the environmental groups with their high-priced lawyers, will always win. If I try to educate the public to the therapeutic physical and emotional benefits of interacting with dolphins in a natural environment (No dolphin zoos/jails, please!), I will inadvertently bring down all the laws to keep me and the children I treat as far away from dolphins as possible.

So, my question is:

"How do we know that it is 'unnatural' for dolphins to want human interaction? How do we know that keeping dolphins and humans separated is natural? How do we know that when we do not allow the dolphins the opportunity to interact with humans in the ocean that we are, by that very action, keeping the dolphins from their 'natural behavior and thereby breaking the law?"

History itself seems at odds with what some marine biologists, environmentalists and federal enforcement officers expect us to accept. Being in the water seems to be natural behavior for me. I have swum with the dolphins for decades. They are my friends. A guest at the Four Seasons once asked me if I talked to all animals or just dolphins. Fact is, I communicate with the rain, the wind, the earth, the ocean, rocks, trees, stars, animals, beings from multiple realities. Oh, and sometimes, humans. The babies especially. It is more that I listen. They all talk to many people, only not many listen.

This was one day that I really wanted to be with my friends. I was experiencing a deep depression; something I had not felt in years. The dolphins had cured me of my disability. When we arrived at the bay, the local kayakers told us "no dolphins today." They had not been in for a few days. My husband assured me they would not be here today. Somehow, I just knew differently. I set up my kayak and my husband and the rest of our group followed. As my husband told us to head out to the far point, I saw my babies. Heading right along the coast, only a couple of hundred yards from shore was a large pod They were calling me and swimming towards me. It took the rest of our group a few minutes to believe me. By the time they followed my lead, I was already surrounded by dolphins. They were under my kayak, in front of me, jumping out of the ocean, and spinning playfully. One of the members of our group excitedly jumped in. The dolphins immediately turned and left. Quiet, gentle entry into the water is the key. There was disappointment in the group, but I assured them they only needed to relax and enjoy the day. The dolphins would come back; they were very active and very much awake on this particular day. The dolphins made a pass around the bay before heading back our way. Ty went in immediately. He always gets the best photos, and the dolphins love him. Once again, the dolphins surrounded us and began leaping everywhere. I relaxed in my kayak, laughing and clapping as the dolphins continued their aerial show. It was so amazingly beautiful. Haleakula rose up out of the island, unusually green from all the rain this season. The ocean ranged from light turquoise and aqua to the deepest blues, all incredibly clear.

We had one young woman with us who had a multitude of physical problems and had recently been released from a hospital. We really did not expect her to get into the water, but you could see that the sun and ocean were relaxing her. She was laughing and clapping at the dolphins. This is it, time to go in. I feel/hear/know when it is time. I turned to look in the direction that their field was calling me and several dolphins were headed my way. I slipped gently into the water and in no time, the dolphins were everywhere. We are sure that there were at least 60 dolphins that day, possibly as many as 80. Some days they are sleeping. When a dolphin sleeps it merely shuts down one side of its brain. That is the way most humans go about their life, using only one side of their brain. When the dolphins look at us, they must think that we are always asleep. Dolphins hunt fish in deep (pelagic) waters at night and then come into the bays to sleep and play. On the days when they are sleeping, being with them is much more trancelike to me. You just swim gently near them, careful not to disturb. They usually have one "awake" dolphin that guides them. The others just follow in their sleep, knowing the "awake" dolphin will be sure they are swimming where it is safe.

Ty finds it amazing that, according to him, I am so gentle and the dolphins trust me so much that they will allow me to be their "awake" dolphin for the pod some days, the closest dolphin nestled up against my arm and shoulder as we swim trancelike through the ocean. The feeling of peace it brings me is indescribable.

"Today they were not asleep," Ty was laughing and telling us, that today was all about sex.

Many dolphins were mating. I always try to stay a bit away and let the dolphins come to me. Today, they loved me. Two came from one direction, two more up underneath me. Suddenly, as I was swimming along, several dolphins joined me. They just sort of "fell in" the way I was going. No doubt today, they were joining me on "my" swim. Spinning and playing, I began spinning with them. Ty was quite upset when I began spinning wildly, splashing everywhere. He had the perfect photo of me with the dolphins and I blew it. Usually, I give him a hard time for lots of dolphin photos, but no humans in them. Today, I did not care. All I wanted to do was play with the dolphins. Two or three at a time would swim right up and appear to kiss my facemask. I knew them, we had played together many times before, this pod and I. As they looked at me, it seemed unmistakable that they knew me as well. They seemed as happy as I was to be there. No matter which direction I would turn to swim, they would follow me. I became elated, filled with blissful joy.

As I surfaced, I heard peals of laughter coming from the woman in our group who had just checked out of the hospital. "Oh My God," she exclaimed. "Ty was right, I am completely surrounded by dolphin sperm!"

She burst into laughter again. It was true, the dolphins were having plenty of sex that day and there were long sperm trails everywhere. Yes, this was truly an all-natural experience. Dolphin sex is quite messy! (Okay, I have been asked many times about dolphin–human sex. I can only tell you that when the dolphins get a little too frisky and start to give me the "hey baby" look; I personally get out of the water. We do have some dolphin-with-dolphin video, showing oral sex, and light stroking with fin of the female organs. Dolphins are not monogamous, but very polite with males patiently waiting in line, in some cases.) Both the woman in the water and I had moved through great depression. She told me that on the trip that day, she felt hope for the first time in a long time. Her depression lifted and to this day, she credits the dolphins for changing the pattern of her depression and shifting her life. Very elated myself, my own depression now gone, I could not have been happier or more content as I started rowing for shore. Swimming with dolphins releases "feel good" endorphins. The dolphins had moved to the far side of the bay. Several tourists were following them, but the dolphins had indicated to me that it was time for us to go. I always pay attention to what the dolphins tell me.

As we approached the shore, it looked from out there like a raid in the parking lot. I had not seen anything like that since the sixties, when I would drive by parties being raided. On this day, there were very intimidating officers standing around, and a multitude of state vehicles. I slowed my kayak and drifted next to my husband.

"Hey look it's a dolphin Raid!"

I have great distance vision, even though I cannot see much up close. As my husband squinted towards the shore, he thought that I was kidding.

"No, sweetie, really. There are cops and state cars everywhere. They even have our truck blocked in."

Sure enough, we came closer to shore and the "environmental cops" were standing on the shore, waiting for the kayakers to come in. More people were seeing the raid now and some kayakers chose to paddle out around the corner. They would leave the ocean farther down the road, avoiding the "dolphin police." The dolphins realized playtime was now over for them and they left the bay. My kayak came perfectly to rest at the feet of the "dolphin police," riding in on a small, but quick, wave. He seemed like a forbidding statue. A tough look on his face, he stared down at me. I smiled up at him.

"I was a good girl. We go to all the NOA meetings."

For just an instant, he smiled at me. That beautiful smile only a true Hawaiian can give, full of gentle aloha. He then gave me a shaka sign and nodded that I should move along. God was blessing me that day. We loaded our kayaks. More than one observer stopped to tell me how lucky I was not to have gotten a ticket. They said the officers had been watching me with binoculars, and it was amazing I had not gotten a ticket. With 30 other people out there that day, my husband said it was impossible to tell who I was in the crowd. That anyone who knew me, knew I would never, ever, harass any cetacean.

I only know that my friends the dolphins came to play with me and no one had decided on that day to take away my rights or the rights of my dolphin friends. Once again, I had witnessed their incredible healing powers in their natural environment and mine—the beautiful ocean. I will always be grateful for that day.

"We play and swim only with Free Dolphins. We ask only to remain Free to do so."

CHAPTER 11
KISSING WHALES

I t was hot on the boat, listening to me lecture. People were antsy and losing their concentration. "Let's jump in and just swim for a few minutes," I said, reaching for my bright yellow fins.

Although everyone had been a bit chilly in the water earlier, they had been very still while practicing treatments in 400-feet of deep, blue, ocean. It was the deepest we had ever gone, quite wild, actually, with the wind and waves coming up. Ty was nervous—unusual for him. I am usually the grandma. I had been with this group yesterday, practicing deep-water treatments in kayaks. The water was so rough we tied one therapist to the kayak and had her hold on to the group so that we would not get lost in the crashing waves. These were advanced girls, two had done over 200 hours training with me and the other two had years of regular ocean swimming experience and were more athletic than me. Now, we were closer to shore in about 150-feet of water (We have a depth finder on the boat and check to see how deep it is if you were wondering. Different depths affect the treatments and the results.). Everyone thought a swimming break a good idea, put on their gear and jumped over with more than one sigh of relief. It would be good for everyone to swim and get their blood moving.

Lyn and Tracy, two Maui therapists in training, took off immediately, both being more comfortable in the open ocean than the other trainees on this trip.

"Don't go too far from the boat and stay fairly close together. We don't need five people floating off in different directions," I said, as Jaye and Marylyn, trainees a bit more nervous in the deep ocean, came close to me. "Good idea, just stick close," I told them, as we swam about 100-yards from the boat. Suddenly, Lyn gestured below her and froze. Marylyn and Jaye moved close enough to hold my hand.

"What's up?" a nervous Jaye enquired.

"Lyn saw something. Stay close to me," I said, checking to see the fastest direction back in the boat.

Tracy had frozen, several feet to the left of, and behind, Lynn. I stuck my head under the water to see what was up. Lynn was moving slowly and carefully backward. Finally, my eyes adjusted and I could just make out the faint reflection of a baby whale playing another 100-yards beyond Lyn.

"Okay, there is a whale in the vicinity. Everyone come close to me and we will keep backing up to the boat."

Unnecessary words for Jaye and Marylyn, who were definitely holding my hand now. I put my face under water waiting for Lyn to get to us, the girls doing the same. This time, a black wall flew past Lyn and right towards us. Before I knew what happened, I was instinctively grabbing tight to the girls, as what seemed like a giant whale flew past. None of us even saw it go, just a black blur. Traci got to us.

"What the heck was that?" she panted.

Lynn made her way to us.

"Everyone get tight, I am not sure what is happening. We will move back to the boat like one big pod."

As we tightened into a human bait ball, we all realized the whale had placed itself between us and the boat, and was just looking at us. We immediately stopped dead in the water. The whale did not move.

"Okay, everyone slowly to the left."

Arms linked, we moved as one, edging slowly straight left. Just like a cartoon, the whale moved exactly the same; still solidly in front of us—still between us and the boat. Then she very slowly started towards us. I have had whales come towards me as if they want to look me in the eye, and I had always managed to hotfoot it back to the boat, so they could only rise out of the water to look me in the eye— which they often do.

For instance, there was the one day that we were having lunch, the boat was turned off and just floating in the current, when four whales surrounded the boat, popping up one at a time to nuzzle against the boat. They held us that way for twenty minutes, rolling one at a time to look at us. Ty calmly munching his sandwich and me with my mouth open. I was afraid if I breathed, they would leave. They all submerged together almost as one, sending me a picture in my mind of myself hanging over the front of the boat, singing to them across the ocean. Wow, they hear me, I thought. They know I am singing for them. At that moment, the whales that had just submerged next to the boat began singing. You could hear it all around the boat above the water, the most beautiful sounds. It saturated my body. I love the whales.

Now, hanging still in the water, I forgot everything except that four-story building moving towards us, very slow, very deliberate.

"It is going to smash us," I thought, "if it doesn't eat us first."

Suddenly, I felt Marylyn reach out her arms, all full of love, and the whale's magnetic field begin to pull her. I grabbed her rubber swim fin and held on tight. Later, she would tell me, "I thought, 'Rebecca is here, we will be all right. Just send the whale love.' Oh MY GOD. I DO LOVE THAT WHALE."

By now, Jaye had climbed on my back with a death grip on my arm.

"I was just trying to get out of the way of the whale," she would laugh later.

In Mexico, Tonga, the Dominican, it is not illegal to actually swim with whales, but you have to realize, under the water, they are immense beings. Feelings range from, "OH MY

GOD, THEY ARE HUGE!" to "I HAVE to get in NOW!"

I had done an experiment once when someone asked me about a whale's pineal gland. I projected myself into a whale's pineal gland and looked around. Sometime later, I would be the first in the water when a whale rushed up to me and, from about 10 feet in front of me, projected itself into MY pineal gland. My pineal gland immediately seemed to expand to about three or four times the size of my entire head. I felt like I was tripping for three days! I never tried that again! In fact, it made me a bit nervous of being in the water face to face. These mammals are a bit too big to slide up my leg the way the dolphins like to do.

My love of the whales is immense too. Once in Hawaii, we were hanging out next to a mom and baby. This particular year, we had five mama whales with new babies that we were checking on, watching out for their safety. Unfortunately, many boat operators are either unaware that so many whales are in the area and drive too fast, or they do not care about Approach Laws in the islands. So, we hang out in the ocean and mamas and babies play close, knowing, I believe, that we will help protect them. Today, a large commercial boat was flying through the water at the mama and baby. I stood up on the boat and began waving at them to go around. They kept flying straight at the mama and baby. They say only the male whales sing. That may be true, but I have heard a mama whale scream when her baby is in trouble. I jumped up on the front of the boat as it came dangerously close to the whales, waving my arms and now shouting. I was pretty hard to miss in my bright red sweatshirt, my husband directly behind me, waving and shouting at the oncoming boat. The other people on our boat were in shock, one woman crying. The big boat, holding over 100 passengers roared right up on top of the whale and baby as they went below the surface. The boat stopped and turned to face us.

"Whales in the area?" the captain asked brightly.

"You just ran over them," I said in shock, watching the

baby whale surface two feet behind the boat in their wake, then just sink back down, no breath.

"See you," the captain smiled and then took off.

"Oh my God! Are you alright? Oh, my God! We are so sorry, so sorry baby," I was crying, leaning out of the boat looking for the whales. "Where are you? Are you alright?"

I could not stop searching for them. Suddenly, the mama surfaced right next to our still turned off boat. She began to dive back and forth from one side of the boat, coming up inches away on the other side. The baby and two other whales joined them. I have never seen anything like it. As they went back and forth, back and forth, you could feel them inside your body. It was like a scan, up and down the inside of our bodies, a scan of unbelievably tangible love. Up and down the inside of our bodies, the gentle, yet powerful, love, zit... zit... zit. . It was as if it was scraping the inside of our bodies; that is the only way I can describe it, but so loving.

Ty stuck his hand into the water with his camera after the whales made what appeared to be the last pass under the boat. Mama whale returned one more time. You could see her rolling her body until her eye was lined up in the lens. Then, as she looked Ty directly in the eye through the camera, she reached with her fin into the boat to touch him. Now, I have seen a lot of things in the ocean with the whales, but this was a first. Everyone in the boat was in tears now, laughing, crying, and hugging each other. It was so clear that the whales knew we had tried to protect them from the oncoming boat, worried about them. They returned our love and passion for them. It was unreal.

I have always been aware of how conscious the whales are, but this was the first time I had seen them use a fin like a hand and reach out to touch someone—SO GENTLE. Yet, in this moment in the middle of the ocean today, as I watched the giant whale watching me, I forget all about everything else, except how BIG it looked. Then, she slowly, steadily, and with obvious intention, moved closer and closer to us. Trust me, if a whale decides to come face to face with you, there is nowhere to go, there's no getting around something that big. The five of us were frozen, hanging in the water in front of her. At some point, as if we were all one being, we laid flat on the surface of the ocean and raised our feet in the air behind and above us. We would all say later that we had done it, as we were afraid our fins would scrape her, if we did not lift them out above the water. As she went under us like the Starship Enterprise, so vast, so slow, it seemed to take forever. She stayed right there, just below us, until her entire body had passed. At some point, my heart burst open and I had to close my eyes. She had moved past us, but apparently turned around and came back. As soon as she passed under us, Traci woke up and bolted for the boat, making it about five feet before she burst into tears. She was watching as the whale turned and twisted her body, moving so that she could reach in between two others to liter-ally reach out and touch me. My eyes were closed; I felt the whale reaching to me.

"If this is real, I can turn my head just a bit, open my eyes, and be looking directly at her fin," I thought.

Even though her fin was right where I expected it to be, coming to my head, it was hard to believe it was real, as it seemed all so, well, unreal. Not until Tracy told me she had seen the whale do it, before I said anything about it myself, could I accept the fact. The whale had reached out to touch me. Not with her biofield. With her hand! (Okay, of course, whales do not have hands; they have fins.)

These days, I live to be in places where the whales are free to swim with us and we are free to swim with them. They are my brothers and my sisters. Even when we are in boats, even when we are a mile or, as I have discovered, thousands of miles, away from them in the water, whales are capable of healing us unlike anything else I have experienced in over thirty years of doing and studying healing.

Their sound heals, their biofield heals, and THEY con-sciously choose to heal us. It is the humpbacks that do this so well. They must have been doing it for a very, very, long time. I can only pray that they continue to teach me and, sometimes, to touch me.

NOTE FROM
THE AUTHOR

Explore Atlantean healing, swim with wild dolphins, or
join me in Tonga to heal and swim with whales.

Contact: P.O. Box 1930, Kihei HI 96753, U.S.A.
cetaceableu@msn.com

SECRETS OF WHALE AND DOLPHIN TREKKING
REVEALED IN MY NEXT BOOK –
"TALES OF A WHALE GROUPIE"
by
Rebecca Goff

www.aquacranial.com

CPSIA information can be obtained
at www.ICGtesting.com
Printed in the USA
BVHW042013061222
653598BV00007B/90